T0209419

An Analysis of

Francis Fukuyama's

The End of History and the Last Man

Ian Jackson
with
Jason Xidias

Published by Macat International Ltd
24:13 Coda Centre, 189 Munster Road, London SW6 6AW.

Distributed exclusively by Routledge
2 Park Square, Milton Park, Abingdon, Oxon OX14 4RN
711 Third Avenue, New York, NY 10017, USA

Routledge is an imprint of the Taylor & Francis Group, an informa business

www.macat.com
info@macat.com

Cataloguing in Publication Data
A catalogue record for this book is available from the British Library.
Library of Congress Cataloguing-in-Publication Data is available upon request.
Cover illustration: Etienne Gilfillan

ISBN 978-1-912303-25-0 (hardback)
ISBN 978-1-912127-91-7 (paperback)
ISBN 978-1-912282-13-5 (e-book)

Notice

The information in this book is designed to orientate readers of the work under analysis,
to elucidate and contextualise its key ideas and themes, and to aid in the development
of critical thinking skills. It is not meant to be used, nor should it be used, as a
substitute for original thinking or in place of original writing or research. References and
notes are provided for informational purposes and their presence does not constitute
endorsement of the information or opinions therein. This book is presented solely for
educational purposes. It is sold on the understanding that the publisher is not engaged
to provide any scholarly advice. The publisher has made every effort to ensure that
this book is accurate and up-to-date, but makes no warranties or representations with
regard to the completeness or reliability of the information it contains. The information
and the opinions provided herein are not guaranteed or warranted to produce particular
results and may not be suitable for students of every ability. The publisher shall not be
liable for any loss, damage or disruption arising from any errors or omissions, or from
the use of this book, including, but not limited to, special, incidental, consequential or
other damages caused, or alleged to have been caused, directly or indirectly, by the
information contained within.

CONTENTS

THE MACAT LIBRARY

The Macat Library is a series of unique academic explorations of seminal works in the humanities and social sciences – books and papers that have had a significant and widely recognised impact on their disciplines. It has been created to serve as much more than just a summary of what lies between the covers of a great book. It illuminates and explores the influences on, ideas of, and impact of that book. Our goal is to offer a learning resource that encourages critical thinking and fosters a better, deeper understanding of important ideas.

Each publication is divided into three Sections: Influences, Ideas, and Impact. Each Section has four Modules. These explore every important facet of the work, and the responses to it.

This Section-Module structure makes a Macat Library book easy to use, but it has another important feature. Because each Macat book is written to the same format, it is possible (and encouraged!) to cross-reference multiple Macat books along the same lines of inquiry or research. This allows the reader to open up interesting interdisciplinary pathways.

To further aid your reading, lists of glossary terms and people mentioned are included at the end of this book (these are indicated by an asterisk [*] throughout) – as well as a list of works cited.

Macat has worked with the University of Cambridge to identify the elements of critical thinking and understand the ways in which six different skills combine to enable effective thinking.
Three allow us to fully understand a problem; three more give us the tools to solve it. Together, these six skills make up the **PACIER** model of critical thinking. They are:

ANALYSIS – understanding how an argument is built
EVALUATION – exploring the strengths and weaknesses of an argument
INTERPRETATION – understanding issues of meaning

CREATIVE THINKING – coming up with new ideas and fresh connections
PROBLEM-SOLVING – producing strong solutions
REASONING – creating strong arguments

To find out more, visit **WWW.MACAT.COM.**

CRITICAL THINKING AND *THE END OF HISTORY AND THE LAST MAN*

Primary critical thinking skill: CREATIVE THINKING
Secondary critical thinking skill: REASONING

Francis Fukuyama's controversial 1992 book *The End of History and the Last Man* demonstrates an important aspect of creative thinking: the ability to generate hypotheses and create novel explanations for evidence.

In the case of Fukuyama's work, the central hypothesis and explanation he put forward were not, in fact, new, but they were novel in the academic and historical context of the time. Fukuyama's central argument was that the end of the Cold War was a symptom of, and a vital waypoint in, a teleological progression of history.

Interpreting history as "teleological" is to say that it is headed towards a final state, or end point: a state in which matters will reach an equilibrium in which things are as good as they can get. For Fukuyama, this would mean the end of "mankind's ideological evolution and the universalization of Western liberal democracy as the final form of human government". This grand theory, which sought to explain the end of the Cold War through a single overarching hypothesis, made the novel step of resurrecting the German philosopher G.W.F. Hegel's theory of history – which had long been ignored by practical historians and political philosophers – and applying it to current events.

ABOUT THE AUTHOR OF THE ORIGINAL WORK

Francis Fukuyama is a professor of political science at Stanford University in the United States and a former advisor to the US government. He was born in Chicago in 1952 to second-generation Japanese immigrants. Fukuyama is part of the intellectual movement that believes the Cold War ended in 1991 with the victory of the West. His controversial theory that Western-style democracy is the pinnacle of human political achievement sparked a storm of public debate that continues to this day.

ABOUT THE AUTHORS OF THE ANALYSIS

Ian Jackson is a PhD student in the Politics, Philosophy and Religion department at Lancaster University. He is interested in the role new media plays in the dissemination of ideas.

Dr Jason Xidias holds a PhD in European Politics from King's College London, where he completed a comparative dissertation on immigration and citizenship in Britain and France. He was also a Visiting Fellow in European Politics at the University of California, Berkeley. Currently, he is Lecturer in Political Science at New York University.

ABOUT MACAT

GREAT WORKS FOR CRITICAL THINKING

Macat is focused on making the ideas of the world's great thinkers accessible and comprehensible to everybody, everywhere, in ways that promote the development of enhanced critical thinking skills.

It works with leading academics from the world's top universities to produce new analyses that focus on the ideas and the impact of the most influential works ever written across a wide variety of academic disciplines. Each of the works that sit at the heart of its growing library is an enduring example of great thinking. But by setting them in context – and looking at the influences that shaped their authors, as well as the responses they provoked – Macat encourages readers to look at these classics and game-changers with fresh eyes. Readers learn to think, engage and challenge their ideas, rather than simply accepting them.

'Macat offers an amazing first-of-its-kind tool for interdisciplinary learning and research. Its focus on works that transformed their disciplines and its rigorous approach, drawing on the world's leading experts and educational institutions, opens up a world-class education to anyone.'

Andreas Schleicher
Director for Education and Skills, Organisation for Economic Co-operation and Development

'Macat is taking on some of the major challenges in university education ... They have drawn together a strong team of active academics who are producing teaching materials that are novel in the breadth of their approach.'

Prof Lord Broers,
former Vice-Chancellor of the University of Cambridge

'The Macat vision is exceptionally exciting. It focuses upon new modes of learning which analyse and explain seminal texts which have profoundly influenced world thinking and so social and economic development. It promotes the kind of critical thinking which is essential for any society and economy. This is the learning of the future.'

Rt Hon Charles Clarke, former UK Secretary of State for Education

'The Macat analyses provide immediate access to the critical conversation surrounding the books that have shaped their respective discipline, which will make them an invaluable resource to all of those, students and teachers, working in the field.'

Professor William Tronzo, University of California at San Diego

WAYS IN TO THE TEXT

KEY POINTS

- Francis Fukuyama is an academic with a background in political philosophy who worked as an analyst at the think tank RAND Corporation* and on the staff of the US government.

- *The End of History and the Last Man* was a response to the collapse of the Soviet Union* in 1991. Fukuyama saw this as the triumph of capitalism* and liberal democracy* and called it the endpoint of history that would replace human conflict with universal peace.

- The text influenced Western foreign policy but has been undermined by world events since publication. It remains under fire from critics who want Fukuyama to update his theory to take into account political changes since 1992.

Who Is Francis Fukuyama?

Francis Fukuyama was born in 1952 to a family of leading academics. His father was a doctor of sociology while his Japanese grandmother founded the economics department of Kyoto University and was the first president of Osaka City University.

Fukuyama followed in their footsteps, studying classics for his Bachelor of Arts degree from Cornell University and political science for his Ph.D. from Harvard. He was taught by influential political thinkers such as Allan Bloom,* Jacques Derrida,* and Samuel Huntington* (who became the fiercest critic of *The End of History*). Fukuyama went on to spark worldwide debate with his controversial theory that political systems shape human history, and that every society moves towards the sole destination of liberal democracy—a political system that emphasizes human and civil rights, free elections between competing political parties and adherence to the rule of law.

Before becoming a career academic, Fukuyama worked as a political analyst at RAND Corporation (Research ANd Development), an American think tank that aims to influence policy through research and analysis. He also worked as deputy director of the Policy Planning Staff at the US Department of State, where he specialized in European and Middle Eastern affairs.

Fukuyama has taught at some of America's leading universities, including Johns Hopkins, George Mason and Stanford, and has worked as a fellow at the Carnegie Endowment for International Peace and the Center for Global Development. He also sits on several powerful academic and non-academic advisory boards, including at the RAND Corporation and the National Endowment for Democracy.

Fukuyama has published a string of important books but his most bold and controversial remains 1992's *The End of History and the Last Man*.

What Does *The End of History And The Last Man* Say?

Francis Fukuyama's grand theory for explaining the post-Cold War* world is that history has a plot, and that its inevitable happy ending is liberal democracy.* He argues that human history is divided up into periods, with each one an improvement on the last. The ultimate destination for everyone is Western-style democracy because that is the best system for satisfying the human need for recognition and equality. When all nations become capitalist democracies, he says, it will mark the end of history.

Fukuyama wrote his landmark book in the immediate aftermath of the Cold War between America and the Soviet Union. *The End of History* was published in 1992, the same year that the Berlin Wall*— the most potent symbol of the East-West divide—was finally demolished. It was also the year after the collapse of the Soviet Union, which ended the global standoff between the two superpowers that had lasted since World War II.

Fukuyama argues that the break-up of the Soviet Union in 1991 proves that liberal democracy and capitalism—an economic system that emphasizes the private ownership of goods—are the best political and economic systems, with the fewest flaws. In *The End of History* he claims that this "triumph of Western liberalism"*—the political philosophy that emphasizes freedom, equality and regularly contested elections—represents a historical endpoint, a final stage that will replace war with lasting, universal peace.

He is not specific about the timeframe for this process. He also acknowledges that some countries face serious obstacles in changing how they operate. But Fukuyama's fundamental argument is that all human societies evolve in the same way, and that human history everywhere leads to liberal democracy.

Fukuyama draws heavily on the ideas of political philosophers of the past in order to build his vision of the future. He revives and develops the famous dialogue between influential nineteenth-century German philosophers Georg Wilhelm Friedrich Hegel* and Karl Marx.* Both thinkers agreed that a historical endpoint would come, but disagreed on what it would be. Hegel's view was that history is a continuing fusion of ideas that lead to refinements in the way society is arranged. This evolution of ideas means that good ideas survive and are, in turn, fine-tuned as people improve society by degrees. Even contradictions, once discovered, lead to further tweaks until spiritual enlightenment is reached. Marx* rejected this idealism and favored a more robust approach to the periodization* of history—one in which revolution brings about meaningful change.

Fukuyama's bold prophesy of the triumph of Western liberalism draws on a wider body of political thought, beyond Hegel and Marx. He is particularly keen on borrowing the concept of *thymos** from the ancient Greek philosopher Plato.* This refers to a part of the human psyche (or soul) that drives people to aim for a fairer, more equal way of life. Plato stated that humans, unlike other animals, require recognition and continually struggle to achieve it. According to Fukuyama, only liberal democracy can satisfy this human need. Another major influence on Fukuyama's writing was Russian-born philosopher Alexandre Kojève,* who offered a twentieth-century interpretation of Hegel and believed that liberalism* was the ultimate—and increasingly universal—stage in world history.

Why Does *The End of History and the Last Man* Matter?

Fukuyama's controversial argument was made at a time of huge uncertainty around the world over the future of international relations. The decades-long Cold War between the United States and the Soviet Union had ended in 1991. The break-up of the Soviet Union left the United States as the last superpower standing, and seemingly the most dominant nation on the planet. Scholars such as Fukuyama and his contemporaries in American universities were attempting to come to terms with this immense change in the balance of world power—and to make difficult predictions about its implications for the future.

From the outset, *The End of History* met with substantial criticism. Fukuyama drew reactions from all parts of the political spectrum and was challenged immediately by equally bold, contrasting viewpoints. The most notable came in *The Clash of Civilizations* written by Fukuyama's former teacher at Harvard, the American political philosopher Samuel Huntington.* For Huntington, the deciding factor in world politics would increasingly boil down to cultural differences. Fukuyama and Huntington were often presented by the media as heading rival "camps," each offering a very different vision of what the future held in store for America and the world.

The End of History and the Last Man remains an important reference point because it had an impact on American and European foreign policy. It is generally agreed that key events since publication undermine the book's core argument (especially the rise of China, which is opposed to liberalism, and the 2008 global financial crisis*). But Fukuyama's outlook remains an inspiration for many politicians. Critics would welcome an updated grand theory in which Fukuyama explains how the reality of the last two decades—including the relative decline of American power, enduring human conflict, and the inability or refusal of some states to implement democratic reforms—fits into humankind's journey to the end of history.

SECTION 1
INFLUENCES

THE AUTHOR AND THE HISTORICAL CONTEXT

KEY POINTS

- Fukuyama argues that the world is moving towards capitalism* and liberal democracy,* and that this is the final stage of history, in which universal peace will replace human conflict.

- He was profoundly influenced by his studies of philosophy as an undergraduate and brought those ideas—along with his experiences working for the think tank RAND Corporation* and the US government—to his predictions for the post-Cold War* world.

- The text was written in the wake of the collapse of the Soviet Union* and at a time when Fukuyama was allied with the neoconservatives*—a branch of American politics devoted to the aggressive imposition of democracy and free-market economics on the rest of the world.

Why Read This Text?

In *The End of History and the Last Man,* Francis Fukuyama sets out to explain America's victory in the Cold War* and what it could mean for the future of relations between states.

According to Fukuyama, capitalism* and liberal democracy,* with their emphasis on civil rights, free elections, and private ownership, will dominate the post-Cold War era. Other systems of government will be abandoned because they do not satisfy the basic human need for recognition and equality. This inevitable spread of liberal democracy is, he says, the endpoint of history and will see human conflict replaced by a commitment to universal human rights.

> **❝** The year 1989—the two hundredth anniversary of
> the French Revolution and of the ratification of the
> US Constitution—marked the decisive collapse of
> communism as a factor in world history ... The Soviet
> Union and PRC [People's Republic of China] turned
> out not to be the atomized, dependent, authority-
> craving children that earlier Western theories projected
> them to be. They proved instead to be adults who could
> tell truth from falsehood, right from wrong, and who
> sought, like other adults in the old age of mankind,
> recognition of their adulthood and autonomy. **❞**
>
> Francis Fukuyama, *The End of History and the Last Man*

Fukuyama's ideas reached beyond traditional academic circles to become part of a wider debate in society and the media. The publication of *The End of History* and the debate that followed have brought the author global fame.

There is an almost undeniable link between the theories Fukuyama sets out in his text, and events in the real world. As John Gray,* a philosopher and critic of Fukuyama, pointed out, "In a span of six years [Tony] Blair* took Britain into war five times,"[1] and [George W.] Bush's* invasion of Iraq* and Afghanistan has cost the United States $1.4 trillion.[2] All of this was done in the name of expanding Western liberal democracy.*

Fukuyama's theory has been debated by academics, politicians and policy-makers and continues to be an important reference point in the study of international relations*—the branch of political science that studies the interactions between states, primarily in terms of their foreign policies.

Author's Life

Francis Fukuyama was born in Chicago in 1952, the only child of second-generation Japanese immigrants. He grew up in New York City then studied for his Bachelor of Arts degree in classics at Cornell University.

At Cornell he studied political philosophy under the noted American thinker Allan Bloom*—the first of a series of scholars who would have a profound effect on his later work. It was Bloom who first introduced him to the ideas of ancient and modern political philosophers, including Plato,* whose ideas became central to Fukuyama's own scholarship.

After Cornell, Fukuyama moved on to graduate studies in comparative literature at Yale University. He spent six months in France, studying poststructuralism*—the idea that language and meaning are shifting and unstable—under influential philosopher and author Jacques Derrida.* But Fukuyama quickly became disillusioned with these studies. He later explained, "Perhaps when you're young you think that something must be profound just because it is difficult and you don't have the self-confidence to say this is just nonsense."[3]

Fukuyama switched to political science, earning a PhD at Harvard University. He studied under Samuel Huntington,* an eminent theorist on post-Cold War politics who later presented the direct counterargument to *The End of History*.

After his PhD, Fukuyama worked for the American economic and foreign policy think tank RAND Corporation* (from 1979–80, 1983–9, 1995–6). He also worked for the policy planning staff of the US Department of State (1981–2, 1989) as well as teaching at the leading American universities Johns Hopkins, George Mason and Stanford. These high-profile roles led to his ideas becoming well-known in politics and the mainstream media.

Author's Background

Fukuyama's background with the US government and the RAND Corporation led to him being considered a neoconservative.* This is a school of thought that promotes the global spread of democracy and free-market economics through a combination of soft power (such as international organizations) and military force.

Fukuyama had worked twice in government with neoconservative politician and academic Paul Wolfowitz;* when Wolfowitz was Dean of the School of Advanced International Studies at Johns Hopkins, he brought Fukuyama in as a professor. This relationship added weight to the suggestion that Fukuyama shared Wolfowitz's political outlook. In 2003, however, he distanced himself from the neoconservative cause by criticizing the administration of US President George W. Bush* and the Iraq War.*

When he wrote *The End of History*, Fukuyama was still working as a consultant for RAND. He was preoccupied with the events of the times: the end of the Cold War, the collapse of the Soviet Union* and the United States' rise to a position of dominance in international relations. These developments followed nearly half a century of simmering tensions between the capitalist* United States and the communist* Soviet Union. Fukuyama drew on a long line of ancient and political philosophy to place the current state of affairs in a historical context, and then make predictions about the future.

The collapse of the Soviet Union largely discredited communism—a political ideology that relies on state ownership, collective labor and the abolition of social class. It led to the view that whatever the merits of Marxist* ideas, they had spectacularly failed in practice. The revolutionary socialist philosopher Karl Marx* had stated that the endpoint of history would arrive when a stateless and classless society finally overthrew capitalism. This would result in a workers' utopia* characterized by absolute freedom. This was never actually achieved by any of the communist states, including the Soviet Union.

Fukuyama identifies a world in which both the communist left and the authoritarian* right revealed "a bankruptcy of serious ideas capable of sustaining the internal cohesion of strong government."[4] According to Fukuyama, every system for organizing society contains fundamental contradictions—except liberal democracy. While still flawed, it does not contain fundamental contradictions—in this sense, at least, it is perfect.

NOTES

1   John Gray, *Black Mass: Apocalyptic Religion and the Death of Utopia* (New York: Penguin, 2007), 97.

2   This figure is probably too low. It does not take into account any interest payable on the money the United States needed to borrow to fund the war. Various opinions place the true cost at somewhere between $2.4 trillion and $3 trillion. Congressional Budget Office, "Iraq and Afghanistan," accessed March 18, 2013, http://www.cbo.gov/topics/national-security/iraq-and-afghanistan/cost-estimates.

3   Cited in Nicholas Wroe, "History's Pallbearer," *Guardian*, May 11, 2002, accessed March 19, 2015, http://www.theguardian.com/books/2002/may/11/academicexperts.artsandhumanities.

4   Francis Fukuyama, *The End of History and the Last Man* (London: Penguin, 2012), 39.

MODULE 2
ACADEMIC CONTEXT

KEY POINTS

- The end of the Cold War* led Fukuyama to argue that Marxism* was utterly defeated and that the spread of capitalist liberal democracy* to all parts of the world was inevitable.

- *The End of History* employs the thoughts of Georg Wilhelm Friedrich Hegel* to approach modern politics. The key notion is that human history moves forward through the evolution of ideas.

- Fukuyama also used Plato's* concept of *thymos**—the struggle for human recognition—to explain political development.

The Work in its Context

The purpose of international relations* has always been to understand and predict state action, and also to have a practical impact on policy. The aim of *The End of History and the Last Man* was to provide a theoretical framework to explain the events unfolding at the time of writing, and to predict the future of global affairs.

In the book, Francis Fukuyama sets out his ideas as to why the Cold War had ended and what would happen next. For him, this was the dawn of an era in which human society would finally settle on one political system—democracy and free market capitalism.*

Fukuyama argues that Marxism—the philosophy of Karl Marx* that had led to communism*—had failed in both China and the Soviet Union.* While a few pockets of communism still remained around the world, on the whole it had vanished as a credible threat to capitalism, the economic system favored by Western liberal democracies.

> ❝ Both Hegel and Marx believed that the evolution of human societies was not open-ended, but would end when mankind had achieved a form of society that satisfied its deepest and most fundamental longings. Both thinkers thus posited an 'end of history:' for Hegel this was the liberal state, while for Marx it was a communist society. This did not mean that the natural cycle of birth, life, and death would end, that important events would no longer happen, or that newspapers reporting them would cease to be published. It meant, rather, that there would be no further progress in the development of underlying principles and institutions, because all of the really big questions had been settled. ❞
>
> Francis Fukuyama, *The End of History and the Last Man*

Fukuyama argues that liberal democracy*—a political system with an emphasis on human rights, regular and free elections and adherence to the rule of law— is the final stage in the evolution of human history, and that it guarantees the triumph of peace over war. Events will still occur, but there will be no progression from liberal democracy to an alternative system because all other systems have been exhausted; they have been tried, and found wanting. As he put it in a 1989 article entitled "The End of History?"*: "What we may be witnessing is not just the end of the Cold War, or the passing of a particular period of post-war history, but the end of history as such: that is, the endpoint of mankind's ideological evolution and the universalization of Western liberal democracy as the final form of government."[1]

Overview of the Field
The End of History stood out in the immediate post–Cold War debate among international relations experts because Fukuyama drew his big ideas from classical philosophy.

Most arguments of the 1990s were between the neorealists* and the neoliberals.* Neorealists believed that all state action springs from the balance of power between states. Neoliberals,* on the other hand, thought that state action is governed by agreed rules of economic cooperation. Fukuyama challenged both these schools of thought by introducing arguments based on classical political philosophy.

Fukuyama's idea of a universal history has its origins in the works of German philosopher Georg Wilhelm Friedrich Hegel,* who was writing in the early 1800s. Hegel believed that history moves through various periods. Each is an improvement on prior eras, so the world moves toward a state of perfection. Marx was greatly influenced by Hegel, and although they predicted different endpoints, they agreed that one would occur.

For Hegel, history is a continuing blend of ideas that leads to refinements in the way society is arranged. Even contradictions prompt changes, until spiritual enlightenment is eventually reached. By contrast, Marx favored revolution as the trigger for meaningful change. He believed revolution would overthrow the oppression and inequality of capitalism and replace it with a stateless and classless society in which workers are free.

Fukuyama also turns to the ideas of Plato, borrowing the ancient Greek philosopher's term *thymos* to describe the engine that drives history.

Thymos describes the part of us that separates us from all other animals (sometimes described as our soul, sometimes as our psyche), identifying it as the desire to be recognized.

For Fukuyama, history is not about understanding a series of events but a series of refinements in the way people organize society. A society must satisfy the needs of its people if it is to survive. Basic needs such as food and shelter must be satisfied, but so must the demands of the *thymos*. Catering for an elusive aspect of the human soul is difficult, argues Fukuyama, so the *thymos* is likely to remain unfulfilled. This will force humanity to strive for perfect political systems.

Academic Influences

The End of History draws on the ideas of Hegel,* Marx, and Alexandre Kojève,* the Russian-born politician and philosopher who coined the phrase "end of history." These thinkers claimed that human history is a long process of social improvements, and that it has an endpoint. To explain constant change, Fukuyama also weaves in Plato's concept of the human pursuit of recognition and equality. Political systems have ranged from aristocratic rule* to fascism* to communism,* says Fukuyama, but only liberal democracy has been able to satisfy the powerful human need and desire dubbed *thymos*.

Once the Cold War had ended, debates over American supremacy and the future of international relations became a feature in numerous publications. Perhaps the most prominent were *Foreign Affairs*—a journal for academics and others involved in international relations; *International Security*—an important outlet for realist* scholars (who believe that states provide for their own security and share the goal of survival) published by the Massachusetts Institute of Technology (MIT) in the United States; and *International Organization*—a platform for liberals produced in Cambridge in the United Kingdom. Fukuyama, however, published the essay that would form the blueprint for *The End of History* in *The National Interest,* a relatively new journal founded in 1985. *The National Interest* was specifically devoted to the question of how America should act on the world stage and promote its own interests abroad. It was less rarefied and more open to Fukuyama's unorthodox ideas than its better-known rivals.

NOTES

1   Francis Fukuyama, "The End of History?" *The National Interest 16* (summer 1989): 4.

MODULE 3
THE PROBLEM

KEY POINTS

- *The End of History* addresses the big question of why liberal democracy* was proving so successful, and whether it could be the final form of human government.

- Fukuyama's ideas were borrowed from leading philosophers of the past, and were applied to how world events might unfold in the aftermath of the Cold War.*

- The terms "the end of history" and "the last man" were taken from philosopher Alexandre Kojève,* who predicted the ultimate triumph of capitalism* and liberal democracy.

Core Question

In *The End of History and the Last Man*, Francis Fukuyama asks why liberal democracy was so successful in the late twentieth century—and whether it marked the end of mankind's ideological evolution by being the final form of human government.

The spread of democracy across the world was a hot topic in the study of international relations during the 1990s, for two reasons:
- The number of liberal democracies hit an all-time high of 61 by 1990.[1]
- The Soviet bloc* collapsed following the end of the Soviet Union* in 1991, with most former Soviet states and all of its satellite states switching to a democratic system.

This created a problem in the field of international relations,* as long-cherished theories had to be hastily rewritten or at least reappraised. For most of the 1970s the theory of détente* (or

> ❝ Of the different types of regimes that have emerged in the course of human history, from monarchies and aristocracies, to religious theocracies, to the fascist and communist dictatorships of this century, the only form of government that has survived intact to the end of the twentieth century has been liberal democracy. ❞
>
> Francis Fukuyama, *The End of History and the Last Man*

"thaw") was an attempt to relax tensions between the United States and the Soviet Union. This was described by Raymond Garthoff* of American think tank the Brookings Institution as a "phase of the Cold War, not an alternative."[2] In the US of the 1980s, under President Ronald Reagan,* détente had been replaced by more open opposition to the Soviet system, but this too had now gone. The world had become unipolar*—only one superpower existed and that was the United States. As America struggled to understand the world it had inherited, a new theory was needed to make sense of this unexpected turn of events.

Fukuyama addresses the big question as to why liberal democracy was winning out in more and more countries by examining it from two angles. First he discusses the economic success of liberal democracies. Then, having concluded that economic factors alone could not explain their rise, he uses a philosophical argument. Fukuyama says that history has an endpoint, and that progress towards this point is driven by the human struggle for recognition—Plato's notion of *thymos*.*

The Participants

Fukuyama's use of philosophy to understand the end of the Cold War was a radically new approach, and his theory should be understood as reintroducing the terms of a much older debate. Other major thinkers tackling the subject, such as Samuel Huntington* and John Mearsheimer,* reacted to his ideas as part of their own attempts to make sense of the emerging new world order. Fukuyama himself, however, looked to the past rather than to his contemporaries for answers.

The end of the Cold War, said historian John Lewis Gaddis, went largely unpredicted by international relations theorists. "Surprise," he said, "is still very much with us," and, "although there was nothing inherently implausible about these events … the fact that they arose so unexpectedly suggests that international relations may need a new approach."[3]

Fukuyama looks to build on earlier theories in order to explain the overall direction of modern-day world politics. The advantage of the free market* (an economy ruled by supply and demand) over a planned economy* (where the government makes all economic decisions) had been evident for some time. Economists such as the Austrian Ludwig von Mises* concluded that the latter system was simply "unworkable" as early as 1935.[4]

Meanwhile, liberal democracies have always considered themselves to be the most evolved way to run a country. Fukuyama's belief that liberal democracy is the culmination of the human quest to find the perfect system of government was also informed by Russian-born French philosopher Alexandre Kojève's writings from the 1940s on.

Kojève's interpretation of Hegel's* "endpoint of history" had a particularly strong influence on Fukuyama's work. It is from Kojève that Fukuyama borrows the term "the end of history," as well as the concept of "the last man." Kojève believed that capitalism and liberal democracy were the final stage in the development of humanity, and that they would result in the equal recognition of all individuals, and the triumph of peace over human conflict.

The Contemporary Debate

Shortly after World War II,* Kojève argued that the United States was the economic model for a "post-historical world"—in other words, a world where all countries would become liberal democracies. He believed that capitalism had overcome its contradictions and that the post-war economic boom in Europe meant the working class could look forward to prosperity. This was in contrast to Marx,* who argued that capitalism would be killed by its contradictions and replaced with communism.*

Long before Fukuyama wrote *The End of History*, Kojève* predicted that the Cold War would lead to the triumph of Western liberalism. This would, he said, produce a historical endpoint that would result in all people being recognized as equals.

This in turn would end the need for war and struggle. Conflict would make way for enduring peace based on a classless, new world order. People would recognize and affirm each other's freedom, and equality would be backed by an elaborate system of law.

Kojève said, though, that the final stage of history would also spell the end of humankind. At the moment of their triumph and the establishment of equality, humans would lose all reason to continue struggling for recognition. This made Kojève's predictions both optimistic and pessimistic. Fukuyama borrows all these ideas and applies them to the post-Cold War era.

NOTES

1 Francis Fukuyama, *The End of History and the Last Man* (London: Penguin, 2012), 50.

2 Raymond Garthoff, *Détente and Confrontation: American-Soviet Relations from Nixon to Reagan (Washington, DC*: The Brookings Institution, 1994).

3 John Lewis Gaddis, "International Relations Theory and the End of the Cold War," *International Security* 17, no. 3 (1992–3): 5.

4 Ludwig von Mises and F. A. Hayek, eds., *Collectivist Economic Planning* (London: Routledge & Kegan Paul, 1935; reprint, Clifton, N. J.: Augustus M. Kelley, 1975), 7.

MODULE 4
THE AUTHOR'S CONTRIBUTION

KEY POINTS

- *The End of History* takes up concepts laid out by earlier philosophers and uses them to create an original theory in a post-Cold War* context.

- The "grand theory" of the work is the shift in attention from victory in war to the triumph of Western liberalism*—it presents a recipe for peace.

- Fukuyama's writings encouraged a reexamination of the influential German philosopher Georg Wilhelm Friedrich Hegel.*

Author's Aims

In *The End of History and the Last Man*, Francis Fukuyama provides an accessible route to understanding political philosophy. He works through ideas in a logical way, explaining both their philosophical background and their political reality. Fukuyama does not assume his readers have any prior understanding and introduces the historical context of ideas before discussing them. He also gives brief biographies of philosophical thinkers and summaries of their work.

The core ideas in the book do not in themselves represent original thought. As French philosopher Jacques Derrida* pointed out in his book *Specters of Marx* (1994): "Eschatological* themes of the end of History, the end of Marxism* … were in the 50s, that is 40 years ago, our daily bread."[1] On the face of it, Fukuyama's theories are entirely borrowed. The concept of an end of history features prominently in Marx* and has its origins in Hegel, while the term itself is closely associated with Alexandre Kojève.*

> 66 With one now-famous essay, Frank Fukuyama did what had hitherto seemed almost impossible: he made Washington think. His subject was, and in this far more sweeping book is, the place of America, and the American idea, in the stream of history. His conclusion is at once exhilarating and sobering. We have won the struggle for the heart of humanity. However, that will not necessarily be good for humanity's soul. 99
>
> George Will, Pulitzer Prize-winning American journalist and political commentator, quoted on the cover of *The End of History and the Last Man*

However, Fukuyama has the insight to draw on the work of earlier thinkers to analyze current events in a meaningful way. He uses established ideas to explain the unexpected collapse of the Soviet Union* and to make sense of a worldwide political landscape that had simply not been envisaged. The impact of such a move was both universal and divisive; that is to say, *The End of History* was widely discussed, but not always in a positive way. Although the work held weight among certain political elites who shared its outlook, of greater significance was the debate it provoked.

Approach

Fukuyama produces a persuasive argument as to why liberal democracies seem to be so much more successful than other forms of government. He also provides a theoretical framework to explain why the Soviet Union had collapsed—one that goes beyond the economic reasons, which Austrian economist Ludwig von Mises* had correctly predicted six decades earlier.[2] For this reason Fukuyama's ideas have been very useful for both students and academics studying post-Cold War* politics. *The End of History* is an up-to-date theory that competes directly with Marxist thinking.* Fukuyama also lays out a believable explanation for the global political realities of the day.

Fukuyama's approach challenged the way in which the Cold War was discussed—that is, mainly in terms of geopolitical and economic competition between the United States and Soviet Union. His grand theory was designed to shift the focus of international relations* away from having won the Cold War, and towards the peaceful but decisive triumph of Western liberalism over all competing systems.

Contribution in Context

The end of history had been discussed at great length by Hegel and Marx, and revived by scholars such as Alexandre Kojève and American sociologist Daniel Bell* in the early stages of the Cold War. But by the time Fukuyama was writing *The End of History*, Hegel's ideas had become quite unfashionable in academic circles. By using them as a foundation for his grand theory about where the post-Cold War world was heading, Fukuyama brought them back into the contemporary debate.

The book had its roots in Fukuyama's 1989 essay "The End of History?"* In this, he observed that analyses of the end of the Cold War lacked "any larger conceptual framework for distinguishing between what is essential and what is contingent or accidental in world history, and are predictably superficial."[3] The essay triggered heated debate, but it was the subsequent book—written largely in response to the furore over the essay—that fleshed out the theory and secured Fukuyama's reputation as a leading thinker in international relations.[4]

The book proved even more divisive than the essay that inspired it. Martin Griffiths* of Flinders University in Australia noted, "[Cambridge professor] John Dunn described it as a 'puerile volume' and [compared] it to 'the worst sort of American undergraduate term-paper.'"[5] In stark contrast, Wayne Cristaudo* of Charles Darwin University judged it to be "the most important defense of liberal democracy since John Rawls's* *A Theory of Justice*."[6]

Whatever waves the book caused at the time, the West did seem to be in the ascendancy in geopolitical terms. Derrida, who was critical of the book's generally positive reception by the Western media, argued that it was "sought out by those who celebrate the triumph of liberal capitalism* ... only in order to hide ... the fact that this triumph has never been so critical, fragile, threatened, even in certain regards catastrophic."[7]

NOTES

1   Jacques Derrida, Specters of Marx: The State of the Debt, the Work of Mourning, and the New International, trans. Peggy Kamuf (New York: Routledge, 1994), 14.

2   Ludwig von Mises and F. A. Hayek, eds., *Collectivist Economic Planning* (London: Routledge & Kegan Paul, 1935; reprint, Clifton, N. J.: Augustus M. Kelley, 1975), 18–22. Mises believed that the mathematics required to predict the needs of the consumer correctly were far too complex to allow for a workable command economy (the sort of planned economy that exists in communist states). Without the law of supply and demand, central governments would be unable to regulate the economy. His theories were validated within the Soviet Union, which encountered all the problems that he had predicted.

3   Francis Fukuyama, "The End of History?", *The National Interest* 16 (Summer 1989): 3–18.

4   Jenefer Curtis, review of *After History? Francis Fukuyama and His Critics*, ed. Timothy Burns, Canadian Journal of Political Science 28, no. 3 (1995): 591.

5   Martin Griffiths et al., Fifty Key Thinkers in International Relations, second ed. (Abingdon: Routledge, 2009), 81.

6   Griffiths et al., Fifty Key Thinkers in International Relations, 82–83.

7   Jacques Derrida, Specters of Marx (New York: Routledge, 1994),15.

SECTION 2
IDEAS

MAIN IDEAS

KEY POINTS

- Fukuyama believes that history is an evolutionary process of human refinement and has an endpoint.

- Capitalism* and liberal democracy* are that endpoint of history. They have won the "clash of ideologies," as all other systems have proved incapable of meeting the human need for recognition and equality.

- In time, every part of the world will reach the same ideological endpoint and become a liberal democracy.

Key Themes

In *The End of History and the Last Man*, Francis Fukuyama focuses on three main themes within one primary idea—the logic of history, which he borrows from Hegel.* In his introduction to the book, he writes that history should be "understood as a single coherent evolutionary process ... taking into account the experience of all peoples in all times."[1]

For Hegel and everyone influenced by him (including Karl Marx,* Alexandre Kojève,* and Fukuyama himself), history is not simply a sequence of events. History is a grand story with a plot—it has a beginning, a middle, and an end. It is the process that drives human societies from where they are to a position that is objectively better. Hegel and his followers defined "better" in terms of freedom. "The history of the world," Hegel wrote in *The Philosophy of History*, "is none other than the progress of the consciousness of freedom."[2]

Fukuyama's grand theory for understanding world politics after the Cold War* has three main themes. First, he stresses that human

> 66 Liberal democracy replaces the irrational desire to be recognized as greater than others with a rational desire to be recognized as equal. A world made up of liberal democracies, then, should have much less incentive for war, since all nations would reciprocally recognize one another's legitimacy. 99
>
> Francis Fukuyama, *The End of History and the Last Man*

society evolves over time, with each stage usually attaining greater freedom than the last. This is based on Plato's* concept of *thymos*,* which sets people apart from animals on the basis of their desire for recognition and equality.

Second, Fukuyama argues that the driving force behind this evolution can only be satisfied by a liberal democratic state, because its emphasis on civil and human rights encourages humans to struggle for recognition, and eventually to recognize each other's freedoms and respect one another's equality. Fukuyama concludes that all other systems, including Marxism,* had failed to achieve this.

Third, he argues that liberal democracy marks the end of history for human society and political ideas, with the "last man" being the triumphant citizen of this system.

Exploring the Ideas

Political scientist Peter Singer* provides an excellent model for understanding the Hegelian view of history that Francis Fukuyama relies on in *The End of History*. In ancient Egypt, Singer writes, only the pharaoh was free and all others subordinated themselves to his will. In the ancient Greek city-states, the citizens were free, and recognized one another as free and equal.[3] This made ancient Greece superior, in that era, to ancient Egypt in terms of social and cultural evolution. While there were still pharaohs in Egypt right up until Roman times,

Hegel would see the Greeks and Romans as having possessed greater freedom, and therefore further along the path of history. This is where *thymos* comes into play. It is the driving force behind this human desire to be recognized as free, equal and worthy of consideration.

The notion that history is propelled by *thymos* feeds Fukuyama's second main idea: that liberal democracies represent the final stage of political development. "As mankind approaches the millennium," Fukuyama writes, "the twin crises of authoritarianism* and socialist central planning have left only one competitor standing in the ring as an ideology of potentially universal validity: liberal democracy, the doctrine of individual freedom and popular sovereignty."[4] Liberal democracy, in other words, is the ideology that most perfectly expresses *thymos*, because it is based on the idea that all people—not just one person or a certain group—are recognized as free and equal.

The end of history does not mean a freezing of time; Fukuyama acknowledges that events will continue to take place once this endpoint is reached. But in his view, these will not add up to "history." Since no alternative form of government satisfies *thymos* as well as liberal democracy, none can hope to replace it.

Fukuyama sees liberal democracy, based on the twin pillars of liberty and equality, as the final form of government to which all others will have to adapt. He does not offer a timetable for these final days of history and even acknowledges that setbacks will occur. He simply believes that democracy will inevitably be established across the world.

Language and Expression

Although Fukuyama does not make precise predictions in his book, he does claim to have identified a measurable trend towards what he called the "liberal revolution." This represents "a common evolutionary pattern for all human societies—in short, something like a universal history of mankind in the direction of liberal democracy."[5]

Fukuyama also strikes a cautionary note, acknowledging undeniable "peaks and troughs in this development."[6] He means that any failure of a liberal democratic state, or even "entire region," should not be seen as "evidence of democracy's overall weakness."[7] These warnings are an important rebuttal to the charge that Fukuyama overstates his theory. Put simply, he concedes that the end of history *can* be reversed, but insists that setbacks will prove to be temporary. Liberal democracy remains the ultimate destination for all states.

His choice of language in portraying liberal democracy as the end of history is highly optimistic. This lack of caution, coupled with more recent events that have undermined his thesis, have resulted in serious criticisms of his work.

NOTES

1   Francis Fukuyama, *The End of History and the Last Man* (London: Penguin, 2012), XII.

2   G. W. F. Hegel, quoted in Peter Singer, *Hegel: A Very Short Introduction*, (Oxford: Oxford University Press, 1983), e-book.

3   Singer, *Hegel*, e-book.

4   Fukuyama, *The End of History*, 42.

5   Fukuyama, *The End of History*, 48.

6   Fukuyama, *The End of History*, 48.

7   Fukuyama, *The End of History*, 50.

SECONDARY IDEAS

KEY POINTS

- Fukuyama argues that technology is an engine of historical change, leading to the disappearance of human conflict and the triumph of universal peace.

- The "last man" is a citizen in a liberal democracy* where equality is the norm.

- *The End of History* provides an overview of democratic peace theory*—the idea that democracies share values and don't declare war on each other.

Other Themes

In *The End of History and the Last Man*, Francis Fukuyama explores three themes that are subordinate to his main argument. The first is the power of science and technology to move human history forward. Technology brings the possibility of limitless economic growth, which Fukuyama says will be welcomed by every nation. And, since having a technologically advanced military means having a comparative advantage in international relations, all nations will seek to improve their defense capabilities. Regardless of a country's history or cultural makeup, science will guarantee that all societies become more alike.

Fukuyama's second theme is that all nations will openly support capitalism* and liberal democracy, removing any reason for going to war. This will result in universal peace. Third, with the defeat of Soviet communism,* "the last man" will be stripped of purpose and ambition.

These themes are linked to one another, and to the main argument. Fukuyama insists that history progresses from societies with less freedom to societies with greater freedom. He explores how free

> **❝** The typical citizen of a liberal democracy was a 'last man' who, schooled by the founders of modern liberalism, gave up prideful belief in his or her own superior worth in favor of comfortable self-preservation. Liberal democracy produces 'men without chests,' composed of desire and reason but lacking *thymos*,* clever at finding new ways to satisfy a host of wants through the calculation of long-term self-interest. The last man had no desire to be recognized as greater than others, and without such desire no excellence or achievement was possible. Content with his happiness and unable to feel any sense of shame for being unable to rise above those wants, the last man ceased to be human. **❞**
>
> Francis Fukuyama, *The End of History and the Last Man*

societies assert and maintain their dominance, and ponders what the future will look like once their dominance is achieved. Fukuyama's vision of the future is pessimistic, because he is certain that the absence of an enemy (Soviet communism) will deprive people of their sense of moral superiority. This will result in a deep sense of emptiness and frustration. In the end, the West's Cold War* victory will prove to be its moral defeat, because values will have been replaced by material ambitions for wealth, security, and comfort.

Exploring the Ideas

Francis Fukuyama argued that the universality of science "provides the basis for the global unification of mankind,"[1] but that it is achieved through military competition. The best way to think of this is in terms of weapons technology. Science makes sure that history moves forward, because it "confers a decisive military advantage on those societies that can develop, produce and deploy technology the most efficiently."[2] Fukuyama thought that this would also make sure that non-democratic societies could not keep pace with liberal ones, because they would have no market incentives to keep technology at the cutting edge.

Fukuyama points to the end of the Cold War,* when "one of the chief reasons [for Soviet surrender] was their realization that an unreformed Soviet Union was going to have serious problems remaining competitive, economically and militarily."[3] In other words, when US president Ronald Reagan used computer technology to make a generation of Soviet missiles obsolete, he "shifted the superpower competition into areas like microelectronics and other innovative technologies where the Soviet Union had serious disadvantages."[4] Fukuyama calls this "defensive modernization." The Soviet Union had no choice but to introduce more freedoms, because it was outstripped in technological development by the United States.

For Fukuyama, the post-history world of wall-to-wall liberal democracies is inevitably still some way off, owing to what is known as the development continuum gap.* This is the difference in economic status, and with it levels of industrialization and political maturity, between the world's richest and poorest nations. As states develop and become more democratic, according to Fukuyama, the chief exchanges will become economic. The old rules of power politics, with their focus on conflict, will become irrelevant. "The civil peace," Fukuyama writes, "brought about by liberalism* should logically have its counterpoint in relations between states."[5] He goes on, noting "the fundamentally un-warlike character of liberal societies is evident in the extraordinarily peaceful relations they maintain among one another," in part because they share an ideology that recognizes one another as legitimate, and in part because they compete on a more friendly, economic basis.[6]

The "last man," then, is a fundamentally peaceful creature who has emerged from the periodization*—developmental steps—of history into a post-historical world. He or she is a citizen of a capitalist* democracy where equality is the norm. However, this person is not ideal, being almost *too* satisfied and content. For Fukuyama, "those earnest young people trooping off to law and business school" may represent this "last man."[7] He worries that "for them, the liberal project of filling one's life with material acquisitions and safe, sanctioned ambitions appears to have worked all too well. It is hard to detect great, unfulfilled longings or irrational passions," the kind that move history and inspire greatness, "lurking just beneath the surface of the average first year law associate."[8] In other words, people in post-historical society have no great struggle and no great project. Instead they face an empty lifetime of accumulating money and possessions.

Overlooked

None of these strands in Fukuyama's larger theory constitute original thinking, although he certainly fleshes out some established ideas. The notion that science influences history's direction has its origins in the work of Hegel* and Marx.* The origins of democratic peace theory* can be traced back to eighteenth-century thinkers Immanuel Kant* and Thomas Paine.* As for the last man, such ideas had been debated for quite some time. Hegel, Marx, German philosopher Friedrich Nietzsche* and others had even argued about whether the last man was a desirable concept. Nietzsche, in particular, lamented the coming of the last men as the arrival of "men without chests."

The ideas in *The End of History* are useful to scholars because they explain why Fukuyama believes that liberal dominance is inevitable. The book provides a snapshot of world politics at the time of writing, and also describes what the last man might look like. This allows us to search for evidence of his existence in parts of the world that are approaching or have achieved post-history. By including democratic peace theory in his work, Fukuyama provides an ongoing test of his own theories. This gives students and academics the opportunity to debate his view of the world.

NOTES

1 Francis Fukuyama, *The End of History and the Last Man* (London: Penguin, 2012), 73.

2 Fukuyama, *The End of History*, 73.

3 Fukuyama, *The End of History*, 75.

4 Fukuyama, *The End of History*, 76.

5 Fukuyama *The End of History*, 260.

6 Fukuyama, *The End of History*, 263.

7 Fukuyama, *The End of History*, 336.

8 Fukuyama, *The End of History*, 336.

MODULE 7
ACHIEVEMENT

KEY POINTS

- Fukuyama argues that liberal democracies* are intrinsically stable, and that non-liberal states are a fluke of history.

- Current events, such as continued conflict in the Middle East, Iran's quest for nuclear weapons and the crisis over Ukraine continue to invite criticism of Fukuyama's thesis.

- The economic success of non-liberal China coupled with the fallout from the 2008 global financial crisis challenge the idea that liberal democracy is perfect and inevitable.

Assessing the Argument

Francis Fukuyama's main purpose in *The End of History and the Last Man* is to show the supremacy of a specific political and economic system—that of liberal democracy and a free market economy.* He argues that the move for nations to adopt this system is a permanent upward trend across the globe, ending the "traditional left and right hemisphere[s]" of politics.

Fukuyama sets out to explain why liberal democracy appeared to have won the ideological struggle that had raged throughout the twentieth century. He sees fundamental contradictions in every other political system, mainly that they do not recognize people as equal. For him, it is logical that society should—and inevitably *would*—organize itself along democratic lines.

Fukuyama provides no actual plan for prompting states to adopt liberal and free market principles. Instead he points to the essential stability of liberal states. Since "few totalitarian* regimes could

> ❝ Francis Fukuyama's influential essay 'The End of History?' announced the triumph of liberal democracy and the arrival of a post-ideological world. But was it just a right-wing argument in disguise? And has the demise of utopianism* ushered in a 'sad time'? ❞
>
> Eliane Glaser in the *Guardian*.[1]

replicate themselves through one or more succession crises,"[2] authoritarianism* itself is a "fluke."[3] It stands to reason, he argues, that non-liberal states are an accident of modern history; they are doomed, because they are at the mercy of any event that proves too much for their inbuilt inflexibility. Such states either fall or reinvent themselves as democracies, and existing democracies will endure. A simple mathematical equation reveals the eventual rise of Western ideology. Even democratic governments voted out of office during times of crisis leave behind a constitutional framework.

Achievement in Context

Understanding Fukuyama's achievement requires an understanding of the time and place in which *The End of History* was written. At the beginning of the 1990s, free market economics, combined with liberal democracies, had provided stability and growth where other systems seemed to have failed. Fukuyama was convinced that this trend would continue. He argued that in order to compete with the West, other countries would have to become more like it; and in growing more alike, they would be more peaceful. Fukuyama acknowledged that a few states would oppose this arrangement, such as North Korea, but sooner or later they would see no alternative but to join in.

The problem is that actual world events did not turn out that way. American president George W. Bush* proclaimed a long-term war against terrorism following the 9/11 terrorist attacks in the United States. Competition intensified between Japan and China, and conflict continued in the Middle East. Iran sought nuclear weapons, while Russia and the European Union struggled over Ukraine.

Another issue is that Fukuyama's theories are firmly rooted in Western liberal philosophy. Even though he explains the concepts, he assumes his readers will be familiar with this tradition. Readers must, therefore, have an understanding of this Western bias in order to fully appreciate his work.

Limitations

Fukuyama wrote *The End of History* as a compelling argument as to why liberal democracies were doing so well compared with other ways of running economic and political life. It succeeds in this, but where it failed was in predicting that democracy would continue to dominate the world stage.

The shortcomings of Fukuyama's analysis became even more glaring with the onset of the 2008 global financial crisis,* which shook the foundations of democracies everywhere and exposed their weaknesses. Rising Asian countries such as Japan received a good deal of attention in the book, yet since *The End of History* was published they have been overshadowed by the rise of non-liberal states. China, the biggest, has adopted a blend of state capitalism* and authoritarianism,* and the Chinese Communist Party* regularly condemns Western democratic and legal conditions.

It could be argued, then, that China is championing an alternative model to the West. The introduction of democracy has also failed in troubled places such as Iraq and Syria. This suggests that democracy and the market cannot flourish without a stable state apparatus and the willingness of most people to adopt the "Western system."

Fukuyama has responded to critiques by arguing that, despite these important developments, the world has still made great progress towards liberal democracy,* and holds to his belief that it will continue to be the dominant political structure.[4]

NOTES

1   Eliane Glaser, "Bring Back Ideology: Fukuyama's 'End of History' 25 Years On," *Guardian*, March 21, 2014, accessed March 19, 2015, http://www.theguardian.com/books/2014/mar/21/bring-back-ideology-fukuyama-end-history-25-years-on.

2   Francis Fukuyama, *The End of History and the Last Man* (London: Penguin, 2012), 40.

3   Fukuyama, *The End of History*, 47.

4   Winston Shi, "Francis Fukuyama: End of History Still in Sight Despite China's Rise," *Huffington Post*, July 9, 2014, accessed March 19, 2015, http://www.huffingtonpost.com/winston-shi/francis-fukuyama-end-of-history-_b_5569581.html.

PLACE IN THE AUTHOR'S WORK

KEY POINTS

- *The End of History and the Last Man* is an extension of Fukuyama's 1989 article where he first sets out his idea that world politics are heading in one direction.

- Fukuyama aimed to plug the gap he perceived in the West's understanding of exactly what had just happened with the collapse of the Soviet Union.*

- Since publication, Fukuyama has distanced himself from the neoconservative* branch of American politics, which he once supported.

Positioning

While Francis Fukuyama found fame as the author of *The End of History and the Last Man*, his academic career did not begin in international relations.* His first degree was in classics, and he went on to study comparative literature before eventually turning to politics. In each field, Fukuyama was most fascinated by philosophy.

As a graduate student at Yale University he spent six months in Paris studying poststructuralism under the French philosopher Jacques Derrida.* Poststructuralism is the name given to ideas stemming from continental Europe during the 1960s and 1970s. Structuralism claimed that human beings could be understood by means of various structures or models. Poststructuralism argued that people are complex, making these structures unstable and therefore unreliable.

Fukuyama became disillusioned with complicated postmodern* criticism and chose to transfer from Yale in order to study political

> ❝What we need, then, and what *The End of History* did not supply, is a theory of political development that is independent of economics. State formation and state-building, how this happened historically, the role of violence, military competition, religion, and ideas more broadly, the effects of physical geography and resource endowments, why it happened first in some parts of the world and not in others—these are all components of a larger theory that has yet to be elaborated.❞
>
> Francis Fukuyama, afterword to *The End of History and the Last Man*

science at Harvard. At Harvard he studied for a Ph.D. and in 1981 completed a doctoral dissertation on Soviet foreign policy in the Middle East.[1]

In the eight years between receiving his doctorate and publishing his initial essay, "The End of History?"*, Fukuyama worked for the influential American policy think tank, RAND Corporation, as a policy analyst specializing in the foreign policy of the Soviet Union. It was during this time that his ideas about the end of history crystallized.

Fukuyama's milestone essay drew on his early experiences of studying across three disciplines, and can be seen as a blueprint for his later thinking. It lays out all the key arguments he would use to build the book published three years later.

Integration

In his 1989 article, published in the journal *The National Interest,*[2] Fukuyama argues that a fundamental change in world history had just occurred. He says that while many scholars wanted to understand why international relations seemed to be heading down a more peaceful path, studies about the end of the Cold War* lacked "any larger conceptual framework for distinguishing between what is essential and what is contingent or accidental in world history, and are predictably superficial."[3]

The book *The End of History* was published in 1992 as a grand theory that could identify and explain the forces of history responsible for the march of democracy around the world. It was also Fukuyama's response to the intense debate stirred up by his original essay. The book proved, if anything, even more divisive.[4] In it, he goes beyond the conclusions reached in the essay by establishing a theoretical framework that emphasizes the triumph of capitalism* and liberal democracy* over every other kind of government.

Significance

The End of History is Fukuyama's most important publication, and made him a well-known figure in international relations.* It has been heavily criticized since it appeared in 1992, and has become more vulnerable over time as major events have failed to tally with his world view. Realities such as the rise of non-liberal China and the 2008 global financial crisis* seem at odds with his predictions.

Fukuyama now acknowledges that the reality of current events and the fact that some states show no indication of being on a liberal, democratic path has weakened the case of *The End of History*.

In his later work, especially *State-Building: Governance and World Order in the 21st Century*, Fukuyama has not wavered from his conviction that all states should aspire to a competent, accountable and democratic government. Such governments should promote a strong civil society based on equal rights, and aim to maximize prosperity. He has, however, acknowledged that for weak or failed states, the path towards this goal is sometimes unclear. Major setbacks have meant that liberal democracy has not yet become universal, and peace has not yet triumphed over human conflict.

Fukuyama says troubled countries such as Somalia, Haiti, and the Congo need state-building help in order to secure a liberal, democratic world order. By state-building he means that rich nations, international organizations, and non-governmental organizations should encourage better government. This would reduce threats to democracy such as human rights abuses, humanitarian disasters, and terrorism.

In recent years, Fukuyama has often been associated with neoconservatism,* a school of thought that emphasizes the importance of free-market economics* and the aggressive promotion of democracy through military force. This is largely down to his involvement with The Project for New Democracy, a neo-conservative think tank.* Many people from the project joined the US Administration under George W. Bush.* This involvement did not last long, however, and in his eyes the group distorted the message of The End of History. By 2003 he had distanced himself from the Bush administration, deciding that "neoconservatism as both a political symbol and a body of thought [had] evolved into something that [I] could no longer support," in particular the way it was used to "justify an American foreign policy that overemphasized the use of force and led logically to the Iraq War."*5

NOTES

1   Martin Griffiths et al., *Fifty Key Thinkers in International Relations, second ed.* (Abingdon: Routledge, 2009), 81.

2   Francis Fukuyama, "The End of History?", *The National Interest* 16 (Summer 1989): 3–18.

3   Fukuyama, "The End of History?", 3–18.

4   Jacques Derrida, *Specters of Marx: The State of the Debt, the Work of Mourning, and the New International* (New York: Routledge, 1994), 15.

5   Francis Fukuyama, *America at the Crossroads: Democracy, Power, and the Neoconservative Legacy* (New Haven, C. T.: Yale University Press, 2006). The Iraq War began in 2003 when a coalition led by the United States and Britain invaded Iraq with the aim of overthrowing the existing regime led by Saddam Hussein.

SECTION 3
IMPACT

THE FIRST RESPONSES

KEY POINTS

- *The End of History* sparked criticism from the political left and right; Samuel Huntington* supplied an alternative theory called *The Clash of Civilizations*.

- Fukuyama claimed his theory had been misunderstood, arguing that Huntington underestimated the power of economic development and technology to make all nations more liberal.*

- Fukuyama was accused of failing to recognize or understand why human conflict has endured, or why some states are still not liberal democracies.

Criticism

Fellow academics, leading politicians, and media commentators were quick to respond to Francis Fukuyama's *The End of History and the Last Man*. His theory of liberal democracy* as the end of history drew criticism from across the ideological spectrum. Fukuyama noted contributions "from Margaret Thatcher,* William F. Buckley,* and the *Wall Street Journal** on the right and *The Nation*,* André Fontaine*, Marion Dönhoff* … on the left."[1]

The most important objections to *The End of History* came from scholars in the field of international relations.* Harvard professor Samuel Huntington concluded that the world was not progressing as his former student had claimed it would. In his rival post-Cold War theory, *The Clash of Civilizations*, Huntington argued that Fukuyama lacked a proper understanding of the workings of world politics.

> **❝** I have been contrasted by many observers to my
> former teacher Samuel Huntington ... I agree with
> him in his view that culture remains an irreducible
> component of human societies ... But there is a
> fundamental issue that separates us. It is the question of
> whether the values and institutions developed during
> the Western Enlightenment are potentially universal, or
> bounded within a cultural horizon. **❞**
>
> Francis Fukuyama, *The End of History and the Last Man*

Huntington warned against fuelling overconfidence in American
statesmen, providing them with a false sense of security that ignored
the decline of Western dominance in relation to its rivals. "In the
emerging [post-Cold War] world," Huntington wrote, "Western belief
in the universality of Western culture suffers three problems: it is false;
it is immoral; and it is dangerous."[2]

Huntington stressed that other cultures had other forms of
government that had grown out of their particular histories. Rather
than seeing the promotion of liberal democracy around the world as
liberating, non-Westerners might see its promotion in their home
countries as aggressive and arrogant.[3]

Author's Response

Francis Fukuyama responded to the furore created by the first airing
of his theory in the 1989 essay "The End of History?" with another
article a few months later entitled "A Reply to My Critics," again in
the journal *The National Interest*. In this, he observed that his "real
accomplishment [had] been to produce a uniquely universal consensus,
not on the current status of liberalism,* but on the fact that I was
wrong and that history has not in fact ended."[4] He went on in the
same dismissive vein, stating that "none of the objections that have

been raised to my thesis strike me as decisive, and the ones that might have been decisive were never raised."

At this point it appears that Fukuyama simply did not accept what his critics were saying. His main objection was that he had been misunderstood. He also suspected many people of not reading the entire 16-page article. Rather than retracting his thesis, he expanded it in 1992 with the publication of *The End of History and the Last Man*.

In 1999 Fukuyama penned a direct reply to Huntington, his former teacher and most formidable critic, in the form of an article in *The National Interest* entitled "Second Thoughts: The Last Man in a Bottle." Fukuyama believes that Huntington underestimates the power of "economic development and technological change" to "blur the boundaries between civilizations" and to promote a universal consensus of political values among advanced countries. He also believes that Huntington is wrong to deny that it is possible "to have economic development without a certain degree of value change in a Western"—that is, liberal capitalist—"direction."[5]

Fukuyama's main concern in this article, however, is that the infinite, forward development of natural science will not lead to the end of history, but will "abolish" human nature through bioengineering and pharmacology (genetic modification and drugs).[6] The article is subtitled "The Last Man in a Bottle" because he worries that antidepressants will allow people to forget their *thymos** (the urge to win recognition and equality) and become "last men" without actually finding freedom.

Conflict and Consensus

Fukuyama's critics insisted that current events had undermined his grand end-of-history theory. While some states may appear to be heading down a path of liberal reform, the reality is that many—such as Somalia—are still far from liberal democracy. Somalia's civil war left the country without a working central government and legal system;

the government is unable to control parts of its territory or meet the basic human needs of its people, such as sufficient food, clean water, education, and health services.

In other countries, such as Sudan, human conflict on ethnic, national, and religious lines is still occurring. This is despite attempts by the United States and the West in general to push through reforms using international institutions. Governments in Iraq and Syria have to a significant extent lost their monopoly on the use of legitimate force within their territories. Meanwhile terrorist groups have moved to fill vacuums left by failed or failing states, and now exercise considerable power.

Huntington accused Fukuyama of failing to understand the profound differences between states. How, for example, did Fukuyama account for the breakdown of state borders drawn during the colonial era in Africa? Furthermore, Huntington feared that America's overconfidence in international affairs could have serious consequences for the future of the West.

NOTES

1   Francis Fukuyama, "A Reply to My Critics," *The National Interest* 18 (Winter 1989/90): 21–28.

2   Samuel Huntington, *The Clash of Civilizations and the Remaking of World Order* (London: Simon and Schuster, 2002), 310.

3   Huntington, *Clash*, 66.

4   Fukuyama, "A Reply to My Critics," 21–28.

5   Francis Fukuyama, "Second Thoughts: The Last Man in a Bottle," *The National Interest* 56 (Summer 1999): 5.

6   Fukuyama, "Second Thoughts," 1.

MODULE 10
THE EVOLVING DEBATE

KEY POINTS

- *The End of History* affected the way Western academics and politicians thought about spreading democracy and capitalism to other countries.

- No school of thought emerged around Fukuyama's theory because the idea of liberal democracy* as the goal of human society has been discussed for centuries.

- Fukuyama has not introduced any completely new thinking to international relations,* as academics in other fields have arrived at the same conclusions independently.

Uses and Problems

Away from academia, Francis Fukuyama's *The End of History and the Last Man* was an important reference point for Western leaders and policy makers who shared his view that democracy was desirable and inevitable everywhere. When Bill Clinton was president of the United States, from 1993 to 2001, the US and the United Kingdom tried to spread free market* values to nations with very different political systems and histories. The International Monetary Fund (IMF)* sent agents "to post-communist* lands carrying the same draft constitution in their briefcases. No matter how discrepant the countries they … tried to impose the same model on them all."[2]

These efforts had limited success, however. The increase in the number of liberal states had apparently stalled by the end of the twentieth century. When George W. Bush* became president of the United States in 2001, he set a neoconservative* course that employed less peaceful ways of imposing top-down regime change—specifically

> ❝ Francis Fukuyama's defence of the universalism of western values and institutions is challenged by modern global political realities. ❞
> Professor Talal Asad, "A Single History?" in *Open Democracy*.[1]

the Iraq War* of 2003. This called into question Fukuyama's vision of universal peace. Subsequently President Barack Obama* took office in 2009 and faced challenges to the idea of the relentless spread of democracy from countries such as China, Russia, Iran, and North Korea.

The main problem with *The End of History* is that history itself has not unfolded in the way Fukuyama expected. World events since the book's publication seem to have undermined his theory of a global march towards Western-style democracy. His ideas were old ones brought forward to fit the world of 1992 and were quickly overtaken by events, a fact recognized by many of his fellow academics.

Schools of Thought

The End of History caused a storm of debate when it was published. Pierre Hassner* of the French political research institute Fondation Nationale des Sciences Politiques in Paris agreed that "the current wave of decline in inter-state conflicts and in revolutionary ideologies, particularly in the developed world, is more than an illusion or a temporary fluke."[3]

Samuel Huntington argued that a third wave of democratization had taken place from 1974, sweeping through Latin America and Eastern Europe and including the end of the Soviet Union. But the process was not as irreversible as Fukuyama had thought, said Huntington, because there could also be "reverse waves."[4]

Meanwhile, Marc F. Plattner* of the National Endowment for Democracy saw *The End of History* as "a carefully structured elaboration ... on the problems and prospects of liberal democracy" that drew on "the classics of political philosophy and the works of modern political and social science."[5] This is an important and unifying point. As Hassner noted, fundamental questions about the meaning of war and peace and legitimacy call for "more than a purely political, military, or economic analysis."[6]

Fukuyama's seminal text covers overlapping fields involving several schools of thought—liberalism,* democratic peace theory,* post-humanism* (the belief that technology can permanently alter the nature of humanity) and realism* (the international relations theory that assumes states are self-governing and answer to no higher body, that they all share the same goal of survival and that they provide for their own security). By building on ideas of democracy proposed by the German political scientist Dankwart Rustow,* and drawing on philosophy, Fukuyama positioned himself alongside a number of thinkers such as Michael W. Doyle,* Robert O. Keohane,* Stanley Hoffmann,* and Richard N. Rosecrance.* They all accepted liberalism as a step forward in human evolution (though not all agreed on Fukuyama's concept of an endpoint).

As early as 1970, Rustow was noting the connection between democracies and "certain economic and social background conditions such as high per capita income, widespread literacy and prevalent urban residence."[7] The neorealist* scholar Kenneth Waltz* also spoke of a "new optimism, strikingly similar to the old," where "interdependence was again associated with peace and increasingly with democracy,"[8] indicating that Fukuyama's influence continued to be felt even within a field from which he had distanced himself.

No single school of thought has formed around *The End of History* itself, though it is most closely related to the study of liberalism. Many liberal thinkers agree with the text's central philosophical arguments, and scholars such as Michael Doyle emphasize the essentially progressive nature of history at a geopolitical* level—that is, the combination of geographic and political factors that influence nations.[9]

While Fukuyama's ideas still hold some weight in certain circles, they have not provided a jumping-off point for new thinking. There are two main reasons for this. The text is essentially revisionist in nature; people who hold with its central ideas already held those views when the book was written. Also, the more instinctive elements of Fukuyama's thinking—such as those adopted by the neoconservatives*—have become either unpalatable to recent governments or impossible in the current geopolitical climate.

In Current Scholarship

The End of History and the Last Man proposes two credible theses: that history is an evolutionary process and that the free market represents the most rational form of economic activity. It can, however, be argued that it has not been responsible for any fundamental new thinking outside the field of international relations.

This is because academics in other fields have arrived independently at ideas that mirror Fukuyama's. The Nobel Prize-winning free market economist Milton Friedman* argued that, "Everyone, everywhere, now understands that the road to success for underdeveloped countries is freer markets and globalization."*[10] Similarly, democratic peace theorists such as the American sociologist Dean Babst* shared many of Fukuyama's views on liberal peace.[11] International relations scholar Michael Doyle went so far as to state that, "unusually for international relations," liberalism "can generate law-like hypotheses … that can in principle be disconfirmed."[12] Each of these schools also draws inspiration from thinkers who were around long before Fukuyama. Democratic peace theory, for example, traces its roots back three centuries to the philosopher Immanuel Kant.*

NOTES

1 Talal Asad, "A Single History?", *Open Democracy*, May 5, 2006, accessed March 19, 2015, https://www.opendemocracy.net/democracy-fukuyama/single_history_3507.jsp

2 John Gray, *Black Mass: Apocalyptic Religion and the Death of Utopia* (New York: Penguin, 2007), 83.

3 Pierre Hassner, "Responses to Fukuyama," accessed March19, 2015, http://www.wesjones.com/eoh_response.htm.

4 Samuel Huntington, *The Third Wave: Democratization in the Late Twentieth Century* (Norman: University of Oklahoma Press, 1993).

5 Marc Plattner, "Exploring the End of History," *Journal of Democracy* 3, no. 2 (1992): 118–21.

6 Hassner, "Responses to Fukuyama."

7 Dankwart Rustow, "Transition to Democracy: Towards a Dynamic Model," *Comparative Politics* 2, no. 3 (1970): 337.

8 Kenneth Waltz, "Globalization and American Power," *The National Interest* 59 (Spring 2000): 46–56.

9 Michael W. Doyle, '"Michael W. Doyle on Markets and Institutions," *Theory Talks*, April 15, 2008, accessed March 19, 2015, http://www.theory-talks.org/2008/04/theory-talk-1.html.

10 Nathan Gardels, "Naomi Klein, Read Milton Friedman's Last Interview," *Huffington Post*, October 1, 2007, accessed March 19, 2015, http://www.huffingtonpost.com/nathan-gardels/naomi-klein-read-milton-f_b_66591.html?

11 Dean Babst, "Elective Governments – A Force for Peace," *Industrial Research* (April 1972): 55–58.

12 Michael Doyle, "Reflections on the Liberal Peace and Its Critics," in *Debating the Democratic Peace*, ed. Michael E Brown et al. (Cambridge, MA: MIT Press, 1996), 358–63.

MODULE 11
IMPACT AND INFLUENCE TODAY

KEY POINTS

- Fukuyama's ideas treat history as an evolutionary process that cannot be permanently blown off course by actual events.

- His theory depended on a sustained increase in liberal democracies around the world but it seems that in reality, we are seeing a sustained decline.

- Critics have called for Fukuyama to address modern political and economic developments in order for his theory to be useful in today's world.

Position

The End of History and the Last Man has influenced the political elite of the West. When philosopher and Fukuyama critic John Gray* noted that "universal democracy and the 'War on Terror'* have proved to be dangerous delusions,"[1] he was highlighting an important link between Francis Fukuyama's theoretical framework and events in the real world.

Although Fukuyama distanced himself from the 2003 invasion of Iraq,* two politicians in particular—US President George W. Bush* and British Prime Minister Tony Blair*—seem to have been heavily influenced by the book. Unlike Bush (a neoconservative* to the core who surrounded himself with other neoconservatives), Blair was a neoliberal* (pro free trade, privatization and deregulation to promote economic liberation, but less of an advocate of the aggressive imposition of democracy). Yet he shifted to the neoconservative agenda after the 9/11 terrorist attack* on the United States.

> 66 Francis Fukuyama's ascription to history of a plot and climax is implausible, but the grain of his work is freshly relevant to the post-9/11* world. 99
>
> Stephen Holmes, Professor of Political Science and Law, New York University, in "The Logic of a Blocked History," *Open Democracy*

Blair held the "belief that only one economic system can deliver prosperity in a late modern context," according to Gray.[2] He never doubted that "globalization* … must eventually be complemented by global democracy."[3] A war to plant democracy in infertile soil can be seen as the most important *political* interpretation of Fukuyama's seminal text. War was no longer "a last resort against the worst evils, but an instrument of human progress."[4]

The End of History is deeply rooted in philosophical ideas that many people find unfamiliar. The Cold War left those who lived through it with only a passing understanding of Karl Marx's* basic ideas. Even fewer knew of Hegel* and fewer still had even heard of Kojève.* While the text itself is well known, its meaning and significance, it seems, are not well understood.

The main misunderstanding is often highlighted by Fukuyama himself. The "fall of the Berlin Wall,* the Chinese government's crackdown in Tiananmen Square* and the Iraqi invasion of Kuwait"* were seen as "evidence that 'history was continuing,' and that [he] was ipso facto proven wrong."[5] Such an analysis points to a fundamental misunderstanding of Fukuyama's concept of history as a single, coherent evolutionary process that had little to do with actual events.

Interaction

In *The End of History*, Fukuyama makes bold claims about the nature of history and its ultimate destination. On a very basic level, his theory depends on the increasing, or at least sustained, dominance of liberal democracies.*

Although Fukuyama expected setbacks, it seems that a sustained reversal is actually in effect.[6] Most geopolitical projections place the United States third in terms of nominal Gross Domestic Product (GDP) by 2050, behind China and India, and second in terms of GDP adjusted for purchasing power parity (considered a more accurate measure), still behind China by a considerable margin. The relevance of the text has been diluted by the simple truth that history has not followed the path that Fukuyama prescribed.

Fukuyama has not ignored this observation, noting "growth in per capita output does far more than put larger resources in the hands of states. It stimulates a broad transformation of society and mobilizes a host of new social forces that over time seek to become political actors as well."[7] This idea is important and shows that his ideas are still challenging wider political thinking.

According to Clyde Prestowitz,* founder of Washington think tank The Economic Strategy Institute, China shows that a country does not need to be liberal to be economically successful. Samuel Huntington* felt the East would "increasingly have the desire, the will and the resources to shape the world in non-Western ways."[8] Both men have directly confronted the spirit of Fukuyama's text and, so far, this criticism has the upper hand. Huntington's view appears the most prophetic; China's economy is set to grow for years to come.

Although Fukuyama has reframed the debate to fit today's intellectual and geopolitical climate more effectively, it is hard to avoid the conclusion that *The End of History* needs to take account of events since its publication in 1992 if it is to remain relevant.

The Continuing Debate

Much has been said about the failure of *The End of History* to predict developments on the world stage with any accuracy. But according to Professor Olivier Roy of the European University Institute, establishing a democracy "does not suppose that a society should go through the same historical and cultural process that the West has undergone."[9] The intellectual debate has shifted toward taking a fresh look at the form a liberal society might one day take.

Fukuyama, after "repenting of [his] neoconservative hubris,"[10] concluded that the events of the past two decades did in fact "not mean the end of the end of history, but rather a temporary respite from the end of history."[11] This shows that his position has not so much changed as softened; his ideas are still opposed by the same thinkers, institutions and schools of thought as before. So, without being revised for the twenty-first century, Fukuyama's theory will continue to be undermined by current events and intellectual critiques.

NOTES

1   John Gray, *Black Mass: Apocalyptic Religion and the Death of Utopia* (New York: Penguin, 2007), 29.

2   Gray, *Black Mass*, 94.

3   Gray, *Black Mass*, 99.

4   Gray, *Black Mass*, 99.

5   Francis Fukuyama, *The End of History and the Last Man* (London: Penguin, 2012), xii.

6   PwC, "World in 2050: The BRICs and Beyond: Prospects, Challenges and Opportunities," accessed March 19, 2015, http://www.pwc.com/en_GX/gx/world-2050/assets/pwc-world-in-2050-report-january-2013.pdf., last modified 2013, accessed March 10, 2013.

7   Francis Fukuyama, *The Origins of Political Order: From Prehuman Times to the French Revolution* (New York: Farrar, Straus & Giroux, 2011), 475.

8   Samuel P. Huntington, "The Clash of Civilizations?", *Foreign Affairs* 72 (1993): 26.

9   Olivier Roy, "The End of History and the Long March of Secularisation," *Open Democracy*, May 15, 2006, accessed March 19, 2015, http://www.opendemocracy.net/node/3546.

10 Charles S. Maier, "The Intoxications of History," *Open Democracy*, May 17, 2006, accessed March 19, 2015, http://www.opendemocracy.net/democracy-fukuyama/intoxication_3560.jsp.

11 Maier, "The Intoxications of History."

WHERE NEXT?

KEY POINTS

- Despite pressure for Fukuyama to update his theory, *The End of History* remains an optimistic vision of the future that many find inspiring.

- Scholars will still study Fukuyama's work but many call for him to update his theory to take account of factors such as China, North Korea, Syria, terrorism and new wars around the world.

- Fukuyama has softened his approach without abandoning his theory, conceding that the end of history might take longer and be a more difficult process than he first imagined.

Potential

The End of History and the Last Man is an important text in which Francis Fukuyama uses the ideas of leading political thinkers from earlier eras to explain our own turbulent period of history. For that reason alone the book will continue to be read. However, Fukuyama's ideas do not reflect the realities of our times and need updating in order to tackle what actually happened after the Cold War.*

The end of history may eventually come, but it has certainly not arrived yet. No universal political and economic system has been established and different parts of the world are still torn by ethnic, national, and religious conflict. Instead of seeing the progress of history through such a wide lens, it may be better to understand each national context as unique, and to address it as such—after all, the complexities of nations such as Somalia, Sudan, Iraq, and Syria are very different.

> **❝** One wonders how this 'feel good' thesis is viewed in Asia, Africa and Latin America, where liberal democracies are often fragile at best and where basic human needs are not being met. Even in Western terms this provocative tract seems more attuned to the self-congratulatory 1980s than the problematic years ahead. **❞**
>
> Andrew Pierre, review of *The End of History and the Last Man*, *Foreign Affairs*

Fukuyama's optimistic belief is that human society is on a path of continual improvement toward a more progressive, egalitarian and peaceful future. The world he describes in *The End of History* has not yet arrived and may never do so, but the work offers an important point of scholarly reference and an inspiring vision that many will fight long and hard to see realized.

Future Directions

The End of History will remain a reference point in the fields of international relations* and politics. As an academic argument, it will continue to be scrutinized as a thesis that does not reflect modern realities—scholars are bound to point to the rise of non-liberal China, the ideological challenges of countries such as Iran and North Korea, the influence of factors such as terrorist groups (which often undermine state power over territories) and ethnic, religious, and sectarian struggles in countries such as Iraq and Syria. Such realities contradict Fukuyama's idea that humankind will adopt one method of government; instead, they suggest that conflict will continue to prevent universal peace.

It seems likely that Western politicians will continue to promote capitalism* and liberal democracy* abroad. Despite different approaches, this has been true of US presidents Clinton*, Bush Jr,* and Obama.* It is equally likely that they will be met with resistance, because not everyone shares their beliefs. Many see their doctrines simply as an imperialist tool used by the West to expand its interests.

Summary

In 1992 Fukuyama made a very big prediction—that capitalism and liberal democracy were the eventual destination for all the people of the world. More than a decade later, the 2003 war in Iraq* saw a United States government fail to plant democratic roots in unfertile foreign soil. And yet another decade on from that, bloody conflict is still a grim reality for many people.

The true test of *The End of History*, however, is whether the economic prosperity seen in non-democratic states such as China is sustainable. If China does not become more liberal, the central premise of the book will become even less justifiable, though not necessarily to a fatal degree.

It is possible that Fukuyama's prediction will only come true over a much longer period of time and that the world will indeed end up locked forever in post-history. The problem with extending the time frame is that it massively dilutes the central argument, since no one can predict what the world will look like hundreds of years from now.

The End of History is a philosophical text at heart. Specifically it is a complicated blend of the ideas of Plato* and Hegel.* From Plato, Fukuyama took the concept of *thymos*,* the desire to be recognized as equal to others. From Hegel, he borrowed the idea that history is divided into periods, and eventually reaches an endpoint. By fusing the two, Fukuyama argued that as liberal democracy satisfies *thymos*, history as an evolutionary process of improvement will grind to a halt.

This complexity makes the work strong enough to be applied to events other than the *annus mirabilis* ("year of wonders") of 1989, when, contrary to the expectations of almost all students of the Soviet regime, change came to Eastern Europe by peaceful means. Just as

Fukuyama revived and extended the ideas of Plato and Hegel, it is possible that other scholars will use his arguments in a new context. To Fukuyama, "liberal democracy is one of the by-products of this modernization process, something that becomes a universal aspiration only in the course of historical time."[1] This "wait and see" policy is one that affords a degree of longevity to the central text, but it is nevertheless not infinite.

There is no denying that the changing geopolitical* reality of the world has been a blow to Fukuyama and his supporters. More recently, Fukuyama has argued that the end of history is not about a "universal hunger for liberty in all people," but rather "the desire to live in a modern society, with its technology, high standards of living, health care, and access to the wider world."[2]

Here he is essentially repeating the complaints made by Soviet citizens before the end of the Cold War.* The demands he alludes to seem to chime with people's clamors during the Arab Spring*—the wave of pro-democracy protests between 2010 and 2012.

It is safe to assume that Fukuyama knows that his seminal text now seems less relevant, hence the softening in his approach. The end of history is still on the horizon, but he seems to acknowledge that getting there will be a much more complex process than he first thought.

NOTES

1 Francis Fukuyama, *America at the Crossroads: Democracy, Power, and the Neoconservative Legacy* (New Haven, CT: Yale University Press, 2006), 54.

2 Fukuyama, *America at the Crossroads*, 54.

GLOSSARY

GLOSSARY OF TERMS

Arab Spring: the name given to the series of protests and wars that began across the Arab world towards the end of 2010.

Aristocracy: a system of government in which power is held by the nobility and continued through hereditary succession. Fukuyama argued that aristocratic rule was one of the forms of government that had been consigned to history.

Authoritarianism: a society that is best understood as involving submission to authority and the exercise of authority by a government.

Berlin Wall: a wall that separated communist East and capitalist West Berlin, built in 1961 and effectively taken down in 1989.

Capitalism: an economic system that emphasizes the private ownership of goods.

Chinese Communist Party: the founding and ruling party of the People's Republic of China. It has often criticized Western ideas regarding capitalism and liberal democracy.

Classical realism: a theory of international relations that emphasizes the self-interest of states. Although Fukuyama probably would not identify himself as a realist, many of the foreign policy decisions made by the George W. Bush administration followed this pattern.

Cold War: defined as a military "tension" between the United States and the Soviet Union; there are no exact dates, but the generally accepted view is that it lasted from around 1945 to around 1991.

Communism: a political ideology that relies on state ownership of the means of production, the collectivization of labor, and the abolition of social class. It was the ideology of the Soviet Union (1917–89), and stood in contrast to free market capitalism during the Cold War.

Cyclical history: in this world-view, events repeat themselves, history has no endpoint and thus there can be no last man.

Democratic peace theory: a theory that believes liberal democracies, for reasons of shared values and interdependence, do not wage war on one another.

Détente: an attempt to relax tensions between the two superpowers of the United States and the Soviet Union, which lasted from 1971 until around 1980, when Ronald Reagan* took office as US president.

Development continuum gap: the North/South divide, sometimes referred to as the Brandt line. This is not a strictly geographic line; Australia and New Zealand are, for example, both considered to be global North states, despite being in the southern hemisphere. Essentially, the line splits the world into wealthy and poor nations. Since the poor nations came late to industrialization and nationalism, so too will they come late to post-history.

"The End of History?": an article that Fukuyama wrote for the journal *The National Interest* in 1989, which can be viewed as a blueprint for the later book.

Eschatology: the study of the end of things, including death, judgment, heaven and hell.

Fascism: a right-wing system of government that came to prominence in the twentieth century. It is characterized by authoritarianism (usually dictator-led) and intolerance of difference. Fukuyama argued that fascism was one of the forms of government that had been consigned to history.

Feudalism: the political and economic system of Europe between approximately the ninth and fifteenth centuries, in which people worked and fought for nobles in exchange for protection and the use of land.

Free market economy: an economy that allows the distribution of goods to follow the laws of supply and demand, without interference from government. Under this system the means of production are in private hands.

Geopolitics: government policy based on how political relations between states are influenced by the geographical features of the countries, such as size, location, natural resources, or borders.

Globalization: the process whereby the world becomes more interconnected. Such interconnectedness takes many forms, including economic, political and cultural.

The Gulf War (1990–1991): a military operation against Iraq that was carried out by the United States, with the help of allies. Given that it was a reaction to Iraq's invasion of Kuwait, it is also known as the Iraq–Kuwait War. It was sanctioned by the UN.

Ideological contamination: this occurs when ideas from one culture gain traction in another. Technology remains the most efficient way of achieving this, and consequently, such ideological contamination is accelerated by the use of new media technology.

Imperialism: the subverting of another country's sovereignty through military power.

International Monetary Fund (IMF): the IMF was set up in 1944 and currently contains 188 nation members, all of which contribute to, and can borrow from, a collective pool.

International relations: the study of the relationships between states, including the study of supranational organizations such as the World Bank and other non-government organizations (NGOs).

Iraq War: a conflict that began in 2003 when a coalition led by the United States and Britain invaded Iraq. The aim was to overthrow the existing regime led by Saddam Hussein's Ba'athist party, which was achieved that same year.

Islam: a religion that bases itself on the word of the Qur'an and the teachings of the prophet Mohammed.

Liberal democracy: a political system that emphasizes human and civil rights, regular and free elections between competing political parties, and adherence to the rule of law.

Liberalism: a political philosophy that emphasizes freedom, equality and regularly contested elections.

Marxism: the name ascribed to the political system advocated by Karl Marx.* It emphasized an end to capitalism by taking control of the means of production out of the hands of individuals and placing it firmly into those of central government. Marxism falls into two main camps, structural and humanistic Marxism. Although both follow the teachings of Karl Marx, the former emphasizes that Marxism is a scientific study of objective structures. Humanistic Marxism, as the name suggests, focuses on the human aspects of his theories, which were laid out in his earlier writings.

Nation, The: a weekly American magazine with leftish leanings.

Neoconservatism: a branch of American conservatism that emphasizes the importance of free-market economics and the aggressive promotion of democracy via military force. Neoconservatives are also, generally speaking, neoliberals. Their views can be seen as an offshoot of American conservatism; in relation to *The End of History*, their principal characteristic is that they advocate the imposition of democracy on other states.

Neoliberalism: seen as a generally right-wing stance that was used in relation to politicians such as Margaret Thatcher and Ronald Reagan, it emphasizes free trade, privatization, deregulation and other moves towards economic liberalization.

Neorealism: while realism sees all states as responsible for their own actions, and interested in their own survival, neorealism stresses that structural constraints limit their actions and motivations.

9/11: terrorist attacks on New York and Washington DC by militant Islamist group Al Qaeda, which killed around 3,000 people. The prevalence of terrorism in the world today undermines Fukuyama's thesis. He argued that all nations would become liberal democracies and that universal peace would replace human conflict.

Periodization: an attempt to create a coherent, inclusive account of history using definable periods of time. For both Marx* and Hegel,* this process was finite and had an ultimate endpoint. Although it remains mostly uncontroversial (everyone is used to thinking of history in terms of periods), thinkers such as Hegel and Marx took the idea and used it to predict the future. Marx predicted that the last period would be communism, while Fukuyama claimed it would be liberal democracy.

Planned economy: under this system, a government agency manages economic production and distribution. This existed in the Soviet Union until its collapse in 1991. The Soviet Union's transition from communism and central planning towards capitalism and liberal democracy was the guiding force behind Fukuyama's end-of-history thesis.

Post-humanism: a belief that technology has the capacity to alter the nature of humanity permanently. It is important to understand that although traces of post-humanism can be found in *The End of History*, Fukuyama himself is opposed to it, seeing it as a threat to liberal democracy.

Postmodernism: begins with an assumption that the values, norms and economic conditions to which people are subjected determine each other, rather than having intrinsic properties that can be understood in isolation. It tends to criticize traditional hierarchies of knowledge, meaning, authority, and interpretation.

RAND Corporation: A powerful think tank in the United States that provides research and analysis to the US military. Fukuyama was an analyst at RAND prior to becoming an academic.

Realism: a school of international relations theory that assumes: (1) states represent the highest form of global responsibility (as opposed to any other organizational body), and all states are responsible for themselves; (2) states all share the goal of survival; (3) states provide for their own security.

Realpolitik: the practical, "doable" aspect of politics that exists outside of desirable or popular movements. For example, although a national poll might indicate that the majority of people want substantial cuts in income tax, Realpolitik would prevent this happening if, according to government advisers, it would lead to economic ruin.

Religious wars: the religious wars in Europe took place between the sixteenth and seventeenth centuries. Several wars were fought during this period, and by the time they had ended secular political institutions were firmly in control.

Socialism: a political and economic theory that advocates a system of social organization in which the means of production and distribution are collectively owned.

Soviet Union: A federal republic officially known as the Union of Soviet Socialist Republics that existed between 1917 and 1991. Fukuyama published *The End of History* in response to its disintegration in 1991, which ended the Cold War.

Soviet bloc: This term refers to the communist states of Eastern Europe, including the Balkans, which shared a common ideology during the Cold War. Fukuyama's end-of-history thesis was based around the transition made by these countries from communism to liberal democracy following the collapse of the Soviet Union.

Thymos: for Plato, *thymos* was the aspect of humanity that separates us from all other animals. It can best be understood as the part of the psyche that desires recognition as a human being. Fukuyama argues that human beings require recognition and that liberal democracy alone satisfies that desire.

Tiananmen Square: student protests in China's Tiananmen Square were put down by military force in 1989.

Totalitarianism: a political system in which the state exercises absolute or near-absolute control over society.

2008 global financial crisis: The financial crisis of 2007–8 is considered by many to have been the worst economic downturn since the Great Depression of the 1930s. This instability of the capitalist system and the criticisms the crisis provoked further highlighted the limits of Fukuyama's end-of-history thesis.

Unipolar world: a world in which one power dominates all others.

Wall Street Journal: an American daily newspaper with an emphasis on economic issues.

War on Terror: declared by George W. Bush as a response to the 9/11 terrorist attack in 2001. What began as an attack on Afghanistan was extended to an attack on Iraq in 2003.

World War II (1939–45): a global war between the vast majority of states, including all great powers of the time.

PEOPLE MENTIONED IN THE TEXT

Louis Althusser (1918–90) was a French Marxist and professor of philosophy at the École Normale Supérieure in Paris.

Talal Asad (b. 1932) is distinguished professor of anthropology at City University of New York. His research interests are religion and secularism, Islamic tradition, political theories, and the Middle East.

Dean Voris Babst (1921–2006) was an influential American sociologist.

Benjamin R. Barber (b. 1939) is an American political theorist and author, who wrote the highly successful *Jihad vs. McWorld* in 1996.

Daniel Bell (1919–2011) was an American sociologist and emeritus professor at Harvard University, who made important contributions to the field of post-industrialism.

Tony Blair (b. 1953) was the prime minister of the United Kingdom 1997–2007.

Allan Bloom (1930–92) was an American philosopher. He taught at Cornell University, Yale University and the University of Chicago. He studied under Alexandre Kojève.

William Buckley (1925–2008) was an American conservative and founder of the influential magazine *The National Review*.

George W. Bush (b. 1946) was the president of the United States 2001–9.

Bill Clinton (b. 1946) was president of the United States 1993–2001.

Wayne Cristaudo (b. 1954) is a professor of political science at Charles Darwin University.

Jacques Derrida (1930–2005) was a French philosopher associated with the school of thought known as poststructuralism, which emphasizes the inherent complexity of human beings and thus the instability of social sciences.

Marion Dönhoff (1909–2002) was part of the German wartime resistance to Hitler and later became a journalist.

Michael W. Doyle (b. 1948) is an international relations scholar best known for his work on liberal, democratic peace.

John Dunn (b. 1940) is emeritus professor of political theory at King's College, Cambridge.

André Fontaine (1921–2013) was a French historian and journalist.

Milton Friedman (1912–2006) was an American economist and Nobel Prize winner who taught at the University of Chicago.

John Lewis Gaddis (b. 1941) is professor of military and naval history at Yale University. He is a well-known expert on the Cold War, and suggested that following the collapse of the Soviet Union, a new framework was needed to understand international relations.

Raymond L. "Ray" Garthoff is a senior fellow at the Brookings Institution, an American think tank based in Washington, DC.

John Gray (b. 1948) is an English philosopher who was formerly professor of European thought at the London School of Economics and Political Science. He remains one of Fukuyama's fiercest critics, and tends to think that Fukuyama was wrong in every conceivable way.

Martin Griffiths is Dean of the School of International Studies at Flinders University, Australia.

Pierre Hassner (b. 1933) is research director at the Fondation Nationale des Sciences Politiques in Paris. His theoretical work centers on war and totalitarianism.

Georg Wilhelm Friedrich Hegel (1770–1831) was a German philosopher whose theories heavily influenced Karl Marx. His school of thought, known as German idealism, was in part a reaction to Immanuel Kant's critique of pure reason. Hegel's ideas on history were set out in the 1807 book *The Phenomenology of the Spirit* and later expanded in a series of lectures given in Berlin in 1821, 1824, 1827, and 1831.

Stanley Hoffmann (b. 1928) is an American scholar whose 2002 book *World Disorders: A Troubled Peace in the Post-Cold War Era* charted the redefinition of the role of military intervention in the twenty-first century.

Samuel Huntington (1927–2008) was an American political philosopher who is best remembered for his vision of a post-Cold War world. Many of his ideas are in direct opposition to Fukuyama's.

Immanuel Kant (1724–1804) was a Prussian philosopher. His 1795 essay "Perpetual Peace" can be seen as a starting point for contemporary liberal thought.

Robert O. Keohane (b. 1941) is an American scholar who in his 2002 book *Power and Governance in a Partially Globalized World* drew on ideas surrounding Thomas Hobbes's *Leviathan*, which were similar to Fukuyama's.

Alexandre Kojève (1902–68), though Russian-born, is best remembered as a French politician and philosopher whose interpretation of Hegel has been extremely influential in the field of continental philosophy. It is from Kojève that Fukuyama took the phrase "end of history."

Karl Marx (1818–83) was one of the most influential philosophers of all time and gives his name to the political philosophy Marxism. Marx rejected notions of liberal freedoms, insisting that the only true freedom was equality. With this in mind, an important stage of Marxist history involved a dictatorship wherein the workers would be forcibly reorganized into a system that would ultimately lead to a classless, stateless society.

John Mearsheimer (b. 1947) is professor of political science at the University of Chicago. He argued, in contrast to Fukuyama, that geopolitics among great powers would continue to play an important role following the Cold War.

Friedrich Nietzsche (1844–1900) was a German philosopher whose seminal works included *Beyond Good and Evil* and *Human, All Too Human*. His ideas have a unique place in Fukuyama's work, since he alone saw the suppression of *thymos* as undesirable.

Barack Obama (b. 1961) is the 44th president of the United States. He assumed office in 2009. His foreign policy has championed the spread of liberal democracy.

Thomas Paine (1737–1809) influenced the American War of Independence. Like Kant, he claimed that republics are peaceful, and do not "go to war out of pride."

Plato (fourth century B.C.E.) was an ancient Greek philosopher. Founder of the Academy in Athens, the first university in the Western world, Plato, along with his teacher Socrates and his student Aristotle, laid the foundations of philosophy and science.

Marc F. Plattner is the vice-president for research and studies at the National Endowment for Democracy, co-director of the International Forum for Democratic Studies, and co-editor of the *Journal of Democracy*.

Clyde Prestowitz (b. 1941) is the founder and president of the Economic Strategy Institute, a Washington-based think tank and lobbying group.

Jacques Rancière (b. 1940) is professor of philosophy at the European Graduate School in Saas-Fee, Switzerland, and emeritus professor of philosophy at the University of Paris.

John Rawls (1921–2002) was an American philosopher whose most famous text, *A Theory of Justice*, was published in 1971 to critical acclaim.

Ronald Reagan (1911–2004) was president of the United States 1981–9. He is widely credited in the United States for bringing an end to the Cold War. He was a proponent of spreading capitalism and liberal democracy around the globe.

Richard N. Rosecrance (b. 1930) is an American economist who, in *The New Great Power Coalition* (2001), argued that the United States must use incentives to bring rising nations such as China and Russia into a coalition or risk them adopting "recalcitrant and antagonistic attitudes toward world affairs."

Olivier Roy (b. 1949) is a professor at the European University Institute in Florence, best known for his book *The Failure of Political Islam.*

Dankwart Alexander Rustow (1924–96) is best known for his work in democratization studies.

Peter Singer (b. 1946) is a moral philosopher and professor of bioethics at Princeton University. Singer's work on Hegel helps explain how Hegel envisioned the end of history as a process of continual refinement.

Gáspár Miklós Tamás (b. 1948) is a Hungarian philosopher and one-time member of the Hungarian parliament.

Margaret Thatcher (1925–2013) was prime minister of the United Kingdom 1979–90. She was a proponent of spreading capitalism and liberal democracy around the globe.

Ludwig von Mises (1883–1973) was an influential Austrian economist and founder of what is known as the Austrian school of economics, which tends to focus on the actions of individuals within the wider economic system, regardless of what form that system takes.

Kenneth Waltz (1924–2013) was an American scholar and one of the most influential thinkers in the field of international relations.

George Will (b. 1941) is a Pulitzer Prize-winning American journalist known for his conservative comments on politics.

Paul Wolfowitz (b. 1943) is a neoconservative politician and academic. Formerly Dean of the School of International Relations at John Hopkins University, he has also acted as president of the World Bank and US deputy secretary of defense.

WORKS CITED

WORKS CITED

Acemoğlu, Daron, and James Robinson. *Why Nations Fail: The Origins of Power, Prosperity, and Poverty*. New York: Crown, 2012.

Asad, Talal. "A Single History?" *Open Democracy*, May 4, 2006. Accessed March 19, 2015. https://www.opendemocracy.net/democracy-fukuyama/single_history_3507.jsp.

Babst, Dean. "Elective Governments – A Force for Peace." *Industrial Research* (April 1972): 55–58.

Barber, Benjamin. *Fear's Empire: War, Terrorism, and Democracy*. New York: W. W. Norton, 2003.

Congressional Budget Office. "Iraq and Afghanistan." Accessed March 18, 2013. http://www.cbo.gov/topics/national-security/iraq-and-afghanistan/cost-estimates.

Curtis, Jenefer. Review of *After History? Francis Fukuyama and His Critics*, edited by Timothy Burns. *Canadian Journal of Political Science* 28, no. 3 (1995): 591–92.

Derrida, Jacques. *Specters of Marx: The State of the Debt, the Work of Mourning, and the New International*. Translated by Peggy Kamuf. New York: Routledge, 1994.

Doyle, Michael W. "Michael W. Doyle on Markets and Institutions." *Theory Talks*, April 15, 2008. Accessed March 19, 2015. http://www.theory-talks.org/2008/04/theory-talk-1.html.

"Reflections on the Liberal Peace and Its Critics." *Debating the Democratic Peace*, edited by Michael E. Brown, Sean M. Lynn-Jones, and Steven E. Miller, 358–63. Cambridge, MA: MIT Press, 1996.

Drury, Shadia B. *Alexandre Kojève: The Roots of Postmodern Politics*. New York: St Martin's Press, 1994.

"Which Fukuyama?" *Open Democracy*, June 7, 2006. Accessed March 19, 2015. https://www.opendemocracy.net/democracy-fukuyama/which_3623.jsp.

Elliott, Abrams. "Letter to President Clinton." *Project for the New American Century*, January 26, 1998. Accessed February 19, 2013. http://www.newamericancentury.org/iraqclintonletter.htm.

Fukuyama, Francis. *America at the Crossroads: Democracy, Power, and the Neoconservative Legacy*. New Haven, CT: Yale University Press, 2006.

"The End of History?" *The National Interest* 16 (Summer 1989): 3–18.

The End of History and the Last Man. Twentieth anniversary edition. London: Penguin, 2012.

"The History at the End of History." *Guardian*, April 3, 2007. Accessed March 19, 2015. http://www.guardian.co.uk/commentisfree/2007/apr/03/thehistoryattheendofhist.

The Origins of Political Order: From Prehuman Times to the French Revolution. New York: Farrar, Straus & Giroux, 2011.

"A Reply to My Critics." *The National Interest* 18 (Winter 1989/90): 21–28.

"Second Thoughts: The Last Man in a Bottle." *The National Interest* (Summer 1999): 16–33.

Gardels, Nathan. "Naomi Klein, Read Milton Friedman's Last Interview." *Huffington Post*, May 15, 2011. Accessed March 19, 2015. http://www.huffingtonpost.com/nathan-gardels/naomi-klein-read-milton-f_b_66591.html?

Garthoff, Raymond. *Détente and Confrontation: American-Soviet Relations from Nixon to Reagan.* Revised edition. Washington, DC: The Brookings Institution, 1994.

Gray, John. *Black Mass: Apocalyptic Religion and the Death of Utopia.* New York: Penguin, 2007.

Griffiths, Martin, Steven C Roach, and M Scott Solomon. *Fifty Key Thinkers in International Relations. Second edition.* Abingdon: Routledge, 2009.

Hassner, Pierre. "Responses to Fukuyama." Accessed March 19, 2015. http://www.wesjones.com/eoh_response.htm.

Himmelfarb, Gertrude. "Responses to Fukuyama." Accessed March 19, 2015. http://www.wesjones.com/eoh_response.htm.

Holmes, Stephen. "The Logic of a Blocked History." *Open Democracy*, May 22, 2006. Accessed March 19, 2015. https://www.opendemocracy.net/democracy-fukuyama/history_blocked_3573.jsp.

Houwelingen, Pepijn van. "(Classical) Realism in the 21st Century." Paper presented at Political Studies Association Annual Conference, Edinburgh, March 29, 2010.

Huntington, Samuel P. "The Clash of Civilizations?" *Foreign Affairs* 72, no. 3 (1993): 22–49.

The Clash of Civilizations and the Remaking of World Order. London: Simon and Schuster, 2002.

The Third Wave: Democratization in the Late Twentieth Century. Norman: University of Oklahoma Press, 1993.

Maier, Charles S. "The Intoxications of History." *Open Democracy*, May 17, 2006. Accessed March 19, 2015. http://www.opendemocracy.net/democracy-fukuyama/intoxication_3560.jsp.

Mises, Ludwig von, and F. A. Hayek, eds. *Collectivist Economic Planning*. London: Routledge & Kegan Paul, 1935; reprint, Clifton, N.J.: Augustus M. Kelley, 1975.

Plattner, Marc. "Exploring the End of History." *Journal of Democracy* 3, no. 2 (1992): 118–21.

PwC. "World in 2050: The BRICs and Beyond: Prospects, Challenges and Opportunities." Accessed March 19, 2015. http://www.pwc.com/en_GX/gx/world-2050/assets/pwc-world-in-2050-report-january-2013.pdf.

Roy, Olivier. "The End of History and the Long March of Secularisation." *Open Democracy*, May 15, 2006. Accessed March 19, 2015. http://www.opendemocracy.net/node/3546.

Rustow, Dankwart. "Transition to Democracy: Towards a Dynamic Model." *Comparative Politics* 2, no. 3 (1970): 337–63.

Sestanovich, Stephen. "Responses to Fukuyama." Accessed March 19, 2015. http://www.wesjones.com/eoh_response.htm.

Shi, Winston. "Francis Fukuyama: End of History Still in Sight Despite China's Rise." *Huffington Post* July 9, 2014. Accessed March 19, 2015. http://www.huffingtonpost.com/winston-shi/francis-fukuyama-end-of-history-_b_5569581.html.

Sim, Stuart. *Derrida and the End of History*. Cambridge: Icon Books, 1999.

Tamás, G. M. "Socialism, Capitalism, and Modernity." *Journal of Democracy* 3, no. 3 (1992): 60–74.

Tziarras, Zenonas. "The Sociology of the Arab Spring: A Revolt or a Revolution." *The Globalized World Post*, August 13, 2011.

Virilio, Paul. *The Information Bomb*. London: Verso, 2005.

Waltz, Kenneth. "Globalization and American Power." *The National Interest* 59 (Spring 2000): 46–56.

Wroe, Nicholas. "History's Pallbearer." *Guardian*, May 11, 2002. Accessed March 19, 2015. http://www.theguardian.com/books/2002/may/11/academicexperts.artsandhumanities.

THE MACAT LIBRARY
BY DISCIPLINE

AFRICANA STUDIES

Chinua Achebe's *An Image of Africa: Racism in Conrad's Heart of Darkness*
W. E. B. Du Bois's *The Souls of Black Folk*
Zora Neale Huston's *Characteristics of Negro Expression*
Martin Luther King Jr's *Why We Can't Wait*
Toni Morrison's *Playing in the Dark: Whiteness in the American Literary Imagination*

ANTHROPOLOGY

Arjun Appadurai's *Modernity at Large: Cultural Dimensions of Globalisation*
Philippe Ariès's *Centuries of Childhood*
Franz Boas's *Race, Language and Culture*
Kim Chan & Renée Mauborgne's *Blue Ocean Strategy*
Jared Diamond's *Guns, Germs & Steel: the Fate of Human Societies*
Jared Diamond's *Collapse: How Societies Choose to Fail or Survive*
E. E. Evans-Pritchard's *Witchcraft, Oracles and Magic Among the Azande*
James Ferguson's *The Anti-Politics Machine*
Clifford Geertz's *The Interpretation of Cultures*
David Graeber's *Debt: the First 5000 Years*
Karen Ho's *Liquidated: An Ethnography of Wall Street*
Geert Hofstede's *Culture's Consequences: Comparing Values, Behaviors, Institutes and Organizations across Nations*
Claude Lévi-Strauss's *Structural Anthropology*
Jay Macleod's *Ain't No Makin' It: Aspirations and Attainment in a Low-Income Neighborhood*
Saba Mahmood's *The Politics of Piety: The Islamic Revival and the Feminist Subject*
Marcel Mauss's *The Gift*

BUSINESS

Jean Lave & Etienne Wenger's *Situated Learning*
Theodore Levitt's *Marketing Myopia*
Burton G. Malkiel's *A Random Walk Down Wall Street*
Douglas McGregor's *The Human Side of Enterprise*
Michael Porter's *Competitive Strategy: Creating and Sustaining Superior Performance*
John Kotter's *Leading Change*
C. K. Prahalad & Gary Hamel's *The Core Competence of the Corporation*

CRIMINOLOGY

Michelle Alexander's *The New Jim Crow: Mass Incarceration in the Age of Colorblindness*
Michael R. Gottfredson & Travis Hirschi's *A General Theory of Crime*
Richard Herrnstein & Charles A. Murray's *The Bell Curve: Intelligence and Class Structure in American Life*
Elizabeth Loftus's *Eyewitness Testimony*
Jay Macleod's *Ain't No Makin' It: Aspirations and Attainment in a Low-Income Neighborhood*
Philip Zimbardo's *The Lucifer Effect*

ECONOMICS

Janet Abu-Lughod's *Before European Hegemony*
Ha-Joon Chang's *Kicking Away the Ladder*
David Brion Davis's *The Problem of Slavery in the Age of Revolution*
Milton Friedman's *The Role of Monetary Policy*
Milton Friedman's *Capitalism and Freedom*
David Graeber's *Debt: the First 5000 Years*
Friedrich Hayek's *The Road to Serfdom*
Karen Ho's *Liquidated: An Ethnography of Wall Street*

John Maynard Keynes's *The General Theory of Employment, Interest and Money*
Charles P. Kindleberger's *Manias, Panics and Crashes*
Robert Lucas's *Why Doesn't Capital Flow from Rich to Poor Countries?*
Burton G. Malkiel's *A Random Walk Down Wall Street*
Thomas Robert Malthus's *An Essay on the Principle of Population*
Karl Marx's *Capital*
Thomas Piketty's *Capital in the Twenty-First Century*
Amartya Sen's *Development as Freedom*
Adam Smith's *The Wealth of Nations*
Nassim Nicholas Taleb's *The Black Swan: The Impact of the Highly Improbable*
Amos Tversky's & Daniel Kahneman's *Judgment under Uncertainty: Heuristics and Biases*
Mahbub Ul Haq's *Reflections on Human Development*
Max Weber's *The Protestant Ethic and the Spirit of Capitalism*

FEMINISM AND GENDER STUDIES

Judith Butler's *Gender Trouble*
Simone De Beauvoir's *The Second Sex*
Michel Foucault's *History of Sexuality*
Betty Friedan's *The Feminine Mystique*
Saba Mahmood's *The Politics of Piety: The Islamic Revival and the Feminist Subject*
Joan Wallach Scott's *Gender and the Politics of History*
Mary Wollstonecraft's *A Vindication of the Rights of Woman*
Virginia Woolf's *A Room of One's Own*

GEOGRAPHY

The Brundtland Report's *Our Common Future*
Rachel Carson's *Silent Spring*
Charles Darwin's *On the Origin of Species*
James Ferguson's *The Anti-Politics Machine*
Jane Jacobs's *The Death and Life of Great American Cities*
James Lovelock's *Gaia: A New Look at Life on Earth*
Amartya Sen's *Development as Freedom*
Mathis Wackernagel & William Rees's *Our Ecological Footprint*

HISTORY

Janet Abu-Lughod's *Before European Hegemony*
Benedict Anderson's *Imagined Communities*
Bernard Bailyn's *The Ideological Origins of the American Revolution*
Hanna Batatu's *The Old Social Classes And The Revolutionary Movements Of Iraq*
Christopher Browning's *Ordinary Men: Reserve Police Batallion 101 and the Final Solution in Poland*
Edmund Burke's *Reflections on the Revolution in France*
William Cronon's *Nature's Metropolis: Chicago And The Great West*
Alfred W. Crosby's *The Columbian Exchange*
Hamid Dabashi's *Iran: A People Interrupted*
David Brion Davis's *The Problem of Slavery in the Age of Revolution*
Nathalie Zemon Davis's *The Return of Martin Guerre*
Jared Diamond's *Guns, Germs & Steel: the Fate of Human Societies*
Frank Dikotter's *Mao's Great Famine*
John W Dower's *War Without Mercy: Race And Power In The Pacific War*
W. E. B. Du Bois's *The Souls of Black Folk*
Richard J. Evans's *In Defence of History*
Lucien Febvre's *The Problem of Unbelief in the 16th Century*
Sheila Fitzpatrick's *Everyday Stalinism*

The Macat Library By Discipline

Eric Foner's *Reconstruction: America's Unfinished Revolution, 1863-1877*
Michel Foucault's *Discipline and Punish*
Michel Foucault's *History of Sexuality*
Francis Fukuyama's *The End of History and the Last Man*
John Lewis Gaddis's *We Now Know: Rethinking Cold War History*
Ernest Gellner's *Nations and Nationalism*
Eugene Genovese's *Roll, Jordan, Roll: The World the Slaves Made*
Carlo Ginzburg's *The Night Battles*
Daniel Goldhagen's *Hitler's Willing Executioners*
Jack Goldstone's *Revolution and Rebellion in the Early Modern World*
Antonio Gramsci's *The Prison Notebooks*
Alexander Hamilton, John Jay & James Madison's *The Federalist Papers*
Christopher Hill's *The World Turned Upside Down*
Carole Hillenbrand's *The Crusades: Islamic Perspectives*
Thomas Hobbes's *Leviathan*
Eric Hobsbawm's *The Age Of Revolution*
John A. Hobson's *Imperialism: A Study*
Albert Hourani's *History of the Arab Peoples*
Samuel P. Huntington's *The Clash of Civilizations and the Remaking of World Order*
C. L. R. James's *The Black Jacobins*
Tony Judt's *Postwar: A History of Europe Since 1945*
Ernst Kantorowicz's *The King's Two Bodies: A Study in Medieval Political Theology*
Paul Kennedy's *The Rise and Fall of the Great Powers*
Ian Kershaw's *The "Hitler Myth": Image and Reality in the Third Reich*
John Maynard Keynes's *The General Theory of Employment, Interest and Money*
Charles P. Kindleberger's *Manias, Panics and Crashes*
Martin Luther King Jr's *Why We Can't Wait*
Henry Kissinger's *World Order: Reflections on the Character of Nations and the Course of History*
Thomas Kuhn's *The Structure of Scientific Revolutions*
Georges Lefebvre's *The Coming of the French Revolution*
John Locke's *Two Treatises of Government*
Niccolò Machiavelli's *The Prince*
Thomas Robert Malthus's *An Essay on the Principle of Population*
Mahmood Mamdani's *Citizen and Subject: Contemporary Africa And The Legacy Of Late Colonialism*
Karl Marx's *Capital*
Stanley Milgram's *Obedience to Authority*
John Stuart Mill's *On Liberty*
Thomas Paine's *Common Sense*
Thomas Paine's *Rights of Man*
Geoffrey Parker's *Global Crisis: War, Climate Change and Catastrophe in the Seventeenth Century*
Jonathan Riley-Smith's *The First Crusade and the Idea of Crusading*
Jean-Jacques Rousseau's *The Social Contract*
Joan Wallach Scott's *Gender and the Politics of History*
Theda Skocpol's *States and Social Revolutions*
Adam Smith's *The Wealth of Nations*
Timothy Snyder's *Bloodlands: Europe Between Hitler and Stalin*
Sun Tzu's *The Art of War*
Keith Thomas's *Religion and the Decline of Magic*
Thucydides's *The History of the Peloponnesian War*
Frederick Jackson Turner's *The Significance of the Frontier in American History*
Odd Arne Westad's *The Global Cold War: Third World Interventions And The Making Of Our Times*

LITERATURE

Chinua Achebe's *An Image of Africa: Racism in Conrad's Heart of Darkness*
Roland Barthes's *Mythologies*
Homi K. Bhabha's *The Location of Culture*
Judith Butler's *Gender Trouble*
Simone De Beauvoir's *The Second Sex*
Ferdinand De Saussure's *Course in General Linguistics*
T. S. Eliot's *The Sacred Wood: Essays on Poetry and Criticism*
Zora Neale Huston's *Characteristics of Negro Expression*
Toni Morrison's *Playing in the Dark: Whiteness in the American Literary Imagination*
Edward Said's *Orientalism*
Gayatri Chakravorty Spivak's *Can the Subaltern Speak?*
Mary Wollstonecraft's *A Vindication of the Rights of Women*
Virginia Woolf's *A Room of One's Own*

PHILOSOPHY

Elizabeth Anscombe's *Modern Moral Philosophy*
Hannah Arendt's *The Human Condition*
Aristotle's *Metaphysics*
Aristotle's *Nicomachean Ethics*
Edmund Gettier's *Is Justified True Belief Knowledge?*
Georg Wilhelm Friedrich Hegel's *Phenomenology of Spirit*
David Hume's *Dialogues Concerning Natural Religion*
David Hume's *The Enquiry for Human Understanding*
Immanuel Kant's *Religion within the Boundaries of Mere Reason*
Immanuel Kant's *Critique of Pure Reason*
Søren Kierkegaard's *The Sickness Unto Death*
Søren Kierkegaard's *Fear and Trembling*
C. S. Lewis's *The Abolition of Man*
Alasdair MacIntyre's *After Virtue*
Marcus Aurelius's *Meditations*
Friedrich Nietzsche's *On the Genealogy of Morality*
Friedrich Nietzsche's *Beyond Good and Evil*
Plato's *Republic*
Plato's *Symposium*
Jean-Jacques Rousseau's *The Social Contract*
Gilbert Ryle's *The Concept of Mind*
Baruch Spinoza's *Ethics*
Sun Tzu's *The Art of War*
Ludwig Wittgenstein's *Philosophical Investigations*

POLITICS

Benedict Anderson's *Imagined Communities*
Aristotle's *Politics*
Bernard Bailyn's *The Ideological Origins of the American Revolution*
Edmund Burke's *Reflections on the Revolution in France*
John C. Calhoun's *A Disquisition on Government*
Ha-Joon Chang's *Kicking Away the Ladder*
Hamid Dabashi's *Iran: A People Interrupted*
Hamid Dabashi's *Theology of Discontent: The Ideological Foundation of the Islamic Revolution in Iran*
Robert Dahl's *Democracy and its Critics*
Robert Dahl's *Who Governs?*
David Brion Davis's *The Problem of Slavery in the Age of Revolution*

The Macat Library By Discipline

Alexis De Tocqueville's *Democracy in America*
James Ferguson's *The Anti-Politics Machine*
Frank Dikotter's *Mao's Great Famine*
Sheila Fitzpatrick's *Everyday Stalinism*
Eric Foner's *Reconstruction: America's Unfinished Revolution, 1863-1877*
Milton Friedman's *Capitalism and Freedom*
Francis Fukuyama's *The End of History and the Last Man*
John Lewis Gaddis's *We Now Know: Rethinking Cold War History*
Ernest Gellner's *Nations and Nationalism*
David Graeber's *Debt: the First 5000 Years*
Antonio Gramsci's *The Prison Notebooks*
Alexander Hamilton, John Jay & James Madison's *The Federalist Papers*
Friedrich Hayek's *The Road to Serfdom*
Christopher Hill's *The World Turned Upside Down*
Thomas Hobbes's *Leviathan*
John A. Hobson's *Imperialism: A Study*
Samuel P. Huntington's *The Clash of Civilizations and the Remaking of World Order*
Tony Judt's *Postwar: A History of Europe Since 1945*
David C. Kang's *China Rising: Peace, Power and Order in East Asia*
Paul Kennedy's *The Rise and Fall of Great Powers*
Robert Keohane's *After Hegemony*
Martin Luther King Jr.'s *Why We Can't Wait*
Henry Kissinger's *World Order: Reflections on the Character of Nations and the Course of History*
John Locke's *Two Treatises of Government*
Niccolò Machiavelli's *The Prince*
Thomas Robert Malthus's *An Essay on the Principle of Population*
Mahmood Mamdani's *Citizen and Subject: Contemporary Africa And The Legacy Of Late Colonialism*
Karl Marx's *Capital*
John Stuart Mill's *On Liberty*
John Stuart Mill's *Utilitarianism*
Hans Morgenthau's *Politics Among Nations*
Thomas Paine's *Common Sense*
Thomas Paine's *Rights of Man*
Thomas Piketty's *Capital in the Twenty-First Century*
Robert D. Putman's *Bowling Alone*
John Rawls's *Theory of Justice*
Jean-Jacques Rousseau's *The Social Contract*
Theda Skocpol's *States and Social Revolutions*
Adam Smith's *The Wealth of Nations*
Sun Tzu's *The Art of War*
Henry David Thoreau's *Civil Disobedience*
Thucydides's *The History of the Peloponnesian War*
Kenneth Waltz's *Theory of International Politics*
Max Weber's *Politics as a Vocation*
Odd Arne Westad's *The Global Cold War: Third World Interventions And The Making Of Our Times*

POSTCOLONIAL STUDIES

Roland Barthes's *Mythologies*
Frantz Fanon's *Black Skin, White Masks*
Homi K. Bhabha's *The Location of Culture*
Gustavo Gutiérrez's *A Theology of Liberation*
Edward Said's *Orientalism*
Gayatri Chakravorty Spivak's *Can the Subaltern Speak?*

PSYCHOLOGY

Gordon Allport's *The Nature of Prejudice*
Alan Baddeley & Graham Hitch's *Aggression: A Social Learning Analysis*
Albert Bandura's *Aggression: A Social Learning Analysis*
Leon Festinger's *A Theory of Cognitive Dissonance*
Sigmund Freud's *The Interpretation of Dreams*
Betty Friedan's *The Feminine Mystique*
Michael R. Gottfredson & Travis Hirschi's *A General Theory of Crime*
Eric Hoffer's *The True Believer: Thoughts on the Nature of Mass Movements*
William James's *Principles of Psychology*
Elizabeth Loftus's *Eyewitness Testimony*
A. H. Maslow's *A Theory of Human Motivation*
Stanley Milgram's *Obedience to Authority*
Steven Pinker's *The Better Angels of Our Nature*
Oliver Sacks's *The Man Who Mistook His Wife For a Hat*
Richard Thaler & Cass Sunstein's *Nudge: Improving Decisions About Health, Wealth and Happiness*
Amos Tversky's *Judgment under Uncertainty: Heuristics and Biases*
Philip Zimbardo's *The Lucifer Effect*

SCIENCE

Rachel Carson's *Silent Spring*
William Cronon's *Nature's Metropolis: Chicago And The Great West*
Alfred W. Crosby's *The Columbian Exchange*
Charles Darwin's *On the Origin of Species*
Richard Dawkin's *The Selfish Gene*
Thomas Kuhn's *The Structure of Scientific Revolutions*
Geoffrey Parker's *Global Crisis: War, Climate Change and Catastrophe in the Seventeenth Century*
Mathis Wackernagel & William Rees's *Our Ecological Footprint*

SOCIOLOGY

Michelle Alexander's *The New Jim Crow: Mass Incarceration in the Age of Colorblindness*
Gordon Allport's *The Nature of Prejudice*
Albert Bandura's *Aggression: A Social Learning Analysis*
Hanna Batatu's *The Old Social Classes And The Revolutionary Movements Of Iraq*
Ha-Joon Chang's *Kicking Away the Ladder*
W. E. B. Du Bois's *The Souls of Black Folk*
Émile Durkheim's *On Suicide*
Frantz Fanon's *Black Skin, White Masks*
Frantz Fanon's *The Wretched of the Earth*
Eric Foner's *Reconstruction: America's Unfinished Revolution, 1863-1877*
Eugene Genovese's *Roll, Jordan, Roll: The World the Slaves Made*
Jack Goldstone's *Revolution and Rebellion in the Early Modern World*
Antonio Gramsci's *The Prison Notebooks*
Richard Herrnstein & Charles A Murray's *The Bell Curve: Intelligence and Class Structure in American Life*
Eric Hoffer's *The True Believer: Thoughts on the Nature of Mass Movements*
Jane Jacobs's *The Death and Life of Great American Cities*
Robert Lucas's *Why Doesn't Capital Flow from Rich to Poor Countries?*
Jay Macleod's *Ain't No Makin' It: Aspirations and Attainment in a Low Income Neighborhood*
Elaine May's *Homeward Bound: American Families in the Cold War Era*
Douglas McGregor's *The Human Side of Enterprise*
C. Wright Mills's *The Sociological Imagination*

Thomas Piketty's *Capital in the Twenty-First Century*
Robert D. Putman's *Bowling Alone*
David Riesman's *The Lonely Crowd: A Study of the Changing American Character*
Edward Said's *Orientalism*
Joan Wallach Scott's *Gender and the Politics of History*
Theda Skocpol's *States and Social Revolutions*
Max Weber's *The Protestant Ethic and the Spirit of Capitalism*

THEOLOGY

Augustine's *Confessions*
Benedict's *Rule of St Benedict*
Gustavo Gutiérrez's *A Theology of Liberation*
Carole Hillenbrand's *The Crusades: Islamic Perspectives*
David Hume's *Dialogues Concerning Natural Religion*
Immanuel Kant's *Religion within the Boundaries of Mere Reason*
Ernst Kantorowicz's *The King's Two Bodies: A Study in Medieval Political Theology*
Søren Kierkegaard's *The Sickness Unto Death*
C. S. Lewis's *The Abolition of Man*
Saba Mahmood's *The Politics of Piety: The Islamic Revival and the Feminist Subject*
Baruch Spinoza's *Ethics*
Keith Thomas's *Religion and the Decline of Magic*

COMING SOON

Chris Argyris's *The Individual and the Organisation*
Seyla Benhabib's *The Rights of Others*
Walter Benjamin's *The Work Of Art in the Age of Mechanical Reproduction*
John Berger's *Ways of Seeing*
Pierre Bourdieu's *Outline of a Theory of Practice*
Mary Douglas's *Purity and Danger*
Roland Dworkin's *Taking Rights Seriously*
James G. March's *Exploration and Exploitation in Organisational Learning*
Ikujiro Nonaka's *A Dynamic Theory of Organizational Knowledge Creation*
Griselda Pollock's *Vision and Difference*
Amartya Sen's *Inequality Re-Examined*
Susan Sontag's *On Photography*
Yasser Tabbaa's *The Transformation of Islamic Art*
Ludwig von Mises's *Theory of Money and Credit*

Macat Disciplines

Access the greatest ideas and thinkers across entire disciplines, including

Postcolonial Studies

Roland Barthes's *Mythologies*
Frantz Fanon's *Black Skin, White Masks*
Homi K. Bhabha's *The Location of Culture*
Gustavo Gutiérrez's *A Theology of Liberation*
Edward Said's *Orientalism*
Gayatri Chakravorty Spivak's *Can the Subaltern Speak?*

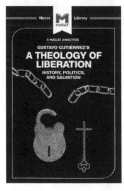

Macat analyses are available from all good bookshops and libraries.

Access hundreds of analyses through one, multimedia tool.

Join free for one month **library.macat.com**

Macat Disciplines

Access the greatest ideas and thinkers across entire disciplines, including

AFRICANA STUDIES

Chinua Achebe's *An Image of Africa: Racism in Conrad's Heart of Darkness*

W. E. B. Du Bois's *The Souls of Black Folk*

Zora Neale Hurston's *Characteristics of Negro Expression*

Martin Luther King Jr.'s *Why We Can't Wait*

Toni Morrison's *Playing in the Dark: Whiteness in the American Literary Imagination*

Macat Disciplines

Access the greatest ideas and thinkers across entire disciplines, including

FEMINISM, GENDER AND QUEER STUDIES

Simone De Beauvoir's
The Second Sex

Michel Foucault's
History of Sexuality

Betty Friedan's
The Feminine Mystique

Saba Mahmood's
The Politics of Piety: The Islamic Revival and the Feminist Subject

Joan Wallach Scott's
Gender and the Politics of History

Mary Wollstonecraft's
A Vindication of the Rights of Woman

Virginia Woolf's
A Room of One's Own

Judith Butler's
Gender Trouble

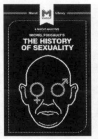

Macat analyses are available from all good bookshops and libraries.

Access hundreds of analyses through one, multimedia tool.

Join free for one month **library.macat.com**

Macat Disciplines

Access the greatest ideas and thinkers across entire disciplines, including

CRIMINOLOGY

Michelle Alexander's
The New Jim Crow: Mass Incarceration in the Age of Colorblindness

Michael R. Gottfredson & Travis Hirschi's
A General Theory of Crime

Elizabeth Loftus's
Eyewitness Testimony

Richard Herrnstein & Charles A. Murray's
The Bell Curve: Intelligence and Class Structure in American Life

Jay Macleod's
Ain't No Makin' It: Aspirations and Attainment in a Low-Income Neighborhood

Philip Zimbardo's
The Lucifer Effect

Macat Disciplines

Access the greatest ideas and thinkers across entire disciplines, including

INEQUALITY

Ha-Joon Chang's, *Kicking Away the Ladder*

David Graeber's, *Debt: The First 5000 Years*

Robert E. Lucas's, *Why Doesn't Capital Flow from Rich To Poor Countries?*

Thomas Piketty's, *Capital in the Twenty-First Century*

Amartya Sen's, *Inequality Re-Examined*

Mahbub Ul Haq's, *Reflections on Human Development*

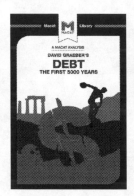

Macat analyses are available from all good bookshops and libraries.

Access hundreds of analyses through one, multimedia tool.

Join free for one month **library.macat.com**

Macat Disciplines

Access the greatest ideas and thinkers across entire disciplines, including

GLOBALIZATION

Arjun Appadurai's, *Modernity at Large: Cultural Dimensions of Globalisation*

James Ferguson's, *The Anti-Politics Machine*

Geert Hofstede's, *Culture's Consequences*

Amartya Sen's, *Development as Freedom*

Macat Disciplines

Access the greatest ideas and thinkers across entire disciplines, including

MAN AND THE ENVIRONMENT

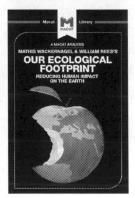

The Brundtland Report's, *Our Common Future*
Rachel Carson's, *Silent Spring*
James Lovelock's, *Gaia: A New Look at Life on Earth*
Mathis Wackernagel & William Rees's, *Our Ecological Footprint*

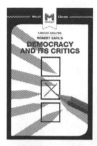

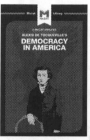

Macat Disciplines

Access the greatest ideas and thinkers
across entire disciplines, including

TOTALITARIANISM

Sheila Fitzpatrick's, *Everyday Stalinism*
Ian Kershaw's, *The "Hitler Myth"*
Timothy Snyder's, *Bloodlands*

Macat analyses are available from all good bookshops and libraries.

Access hundreds of analyses through one, multimedia tool.
Join free for one month **library.macat.com**

Macat Pairs

Analyse historical and modern issues from opposite sides of an argument. Pairs include:

RACE AND IDENTITY

Zora Neale Hurston's
Characteristics of Negro Expression

Using material collected on anthropological expeditions to the South, Zora Neale Hurston explains how expression in African American culture in the early twentieth century departs from the art of white America. At the time, African American art was often criticized for copying white culture. For Hurston, this criticism misunderstood how art works. European tradition views art as something fixed. But Hurston describes a creative process that is alive, ever-changing, and largely improvisational. She maintains that African American art works through a process called 'mimicry'—where an imitated object or verbal pattern, for example, is reshaped and altered until it becomes something new, novel—and worthy of attention.

Frantz Fanon's
Black Skin, White Masks

Black Skin, White Masks offers a radical analysis of the psychological effects of colonization on the colonized.

Fanon witnessed the effects of colonization first hand both in his birthplace, Martinique, and again later in life when he worked as a psychiatrist in another French colony, Algeria. His text is uncompromising in form and argument. He dissects the dehumanizing effects of colonialism, arguing that it destroys the native sense of identity, forcing people to adapt to an alien set of values—including a core belief that they are inferior. This results in deep psychological trauma.

Fanon's work played a pivotal role in the civil rights movements of the 1960s.

Macat Pairs

Analyse historical and modern issues from opposite sides of an argument. Pairs include:

INTERNATIONAL RELATIONS IN THE 21ˢᵀ CENTURY

Samuel P. Huntington's
The Clash of Civilisations

In his highly influential 1996 book, Huntington offers a vision of a post-Cold War world in which conflict takes place not between competing ideologies but between cultures. The worst clash, he argues, will be between the Islamic world and the West: the West's arrogance and belief that its culture is a "gift" to the world will come into conflict with Islam's obstinacy and concern that its culture is under attack from a morally decadent "other."

Clash inspired much debate between different political schools of thought. But its greatest impact came in helping define American foreign policy in the wake of the 2001 terrorist attacks in New York and Washington.

Francis Fukuyama's
The End of History and the Last Man

Published in 1992, *The End of History and the Last Man* argues that capitalist democracy is the final destination for all societies. Fukuyama believed democracy triumphed during the Cold War because it lacks the "fundamental contradictions" inherent in communism and satisfies our yearning for freedom and equality. Democracy therefore marks the endpoint in the evolution of ideology, and so the "end of history." There will still be "events," but no fundamental change in ideology.

Macat Pairs

*Analyse historical and modern issues
from opposite sides of an argument.
Pairs include:*

HOW TO RUN AN ECONOMY

John Maynard Keynes's
*The General Theory OF Employment,
Interest and Money*

Classical economics suggests that market economies
are self-correcting in times of recession or depression,
and tend toward full employment and output. But
English economist John Maynard Keynes disagrees.

In his ground-breaking 1936 study *The General
Theory*, Keynes argues that traditional economics
has misunderstood the causes of unemployment.
Employment is not determined by the price of labor;
it is directly linked to demand. Keynes believes market
economies are by nature unstable, and so require
government intervention. Spurred on by the social
catastrophe of the Great Depression of the 1930s,
he sets out to revolutionize the way the world thinks

Milton Friedman's
The Role of Monetary Policy

Friedman's 1968 paper changed the course of
economic theory. In just 17 pages, he demolished
existing theory and outlined an effective alternate
monetary policy designed to secure 'high employment,
stable prices and rapid growth.'

Friedman demonstrated that monetary policy plays
a vital role in broader economic stability and argued
that economists got their monetary policy wrong
in the 1950s and 1960s by misunderstanding the
relationship between inflation and unemployment.
Previous generations of economists had believed
that governments could permanently decrease
unemployment by permitting inflation—and vice versa.
Friedman's most original contribution was to show that
this supposed trade-off is an illusion that only works in
the short term.

Macat analyses are available from all good bookshops and libraries.

Access hundreds of analyses through one, multimedia tool.
Join free for one month **library.macat.com**

Macat Pairs

*Analyse historical and modern issues
from opposite sides of an argument.
Pairs include:*

ARE WE FUNDAMENTALLY GOOD - OR BAD?

Steven Pinker's
The Better Angels of Our Nature
Stephen Pinker's gloriously optimistic 2011 book argues that, despite humanity's biological tendency toward violence, we are, in fact, less violent today than ever before. To prove his case, Pinker lays out pages of detailed statistical evidence. For him, much of the credit for the decline goes to the eighteenth-century Enlightenment movement, whose ideas of liberty, tolerance, and respect for the value of human life filtered down through society and affected how people thought. That psychological change led to behavioral change—and overall we became more peaceful. Critics countered that humanity could never overcome the biological urge toward violence; others argued that Pinker's statistics were flawed.

Philip Zimbardo's
The Lucifer Effect
Some psychologists believe those who commit cruelty are innately evil. Zimbardo disagrees. In *The Lucifer Effect*, he argues that sometimes good people do evil things simply because of the situations they find themselves in, citing many historical examples to illustrate his point. Zimbardo details his 1971 Stanford prison experiment, where ordinary volunteers playing guards in a mock prison rapidly became abusive. But he also describes the tortures committed by US army personnel in Iraq's Abu Ghraib prison in 2003—and how he himself testified in defence of one of those guards. committed by US army personnel in Iraq's Abu Ghraib prison in 2003—and how he himself testified in defence of one of those guards.

Macat analyses are available from all good bookshops and libraries.

Access hundreds of analyses through one, multimedia tool.

Join free for one month library.macat.com

Macat Pairs

Analyse historical and modern issues from opposite sides of an argument. Pairs include:

HOW WE RELATE TO EACH OTHER AND SOCIETY

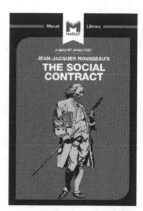

Jean-Jacques Rousseau's
The Social Contract

Rousseau's famous work sets out the radical concept of the 'social contract': a give-and-take relationship between individual freedom and social order.

If people are free to do as they like, governed only by their own sense of justice, they are also vulnerable to chaos and violence. To avoid this, Rousseau proposes they should agree to give up some freedom to benefit from the protection of social and political organization. But this deal is only just if societies are led by the collective needs and desires of the people, and able to control the private interests of individuals. For Rousseau, the only legitimate form of government is rule by the people.

Robert D. Putnam's
Bowling Alone

In *Bowling Alone*, Robert Putnam argues that Americans have become disconnected from one another and from the institutions of their common life, and investigates the consequences of this change.

Looking at a range of indicators, from membership in formal organizations to the number of invitations being extended to informal dinner parties, Putnam demonstrates that Americans are interacting less and creating less "social capital" – with potentially disastrous implications for their society.

It would be difficult to overstate the impact of *Bowling Alone*, one of the most frequently cited social science publications of the last half-century.

Macat analyses are available from all good bookshops and libraries.

Access hundreds of analyses through one, multimedia tool.

Join free for one month **library.macat.com**

Printed in the United States
by Baker & Taylor Publisher Services